Prayers That Avail Much
For Mothers

Prayers That Avail Much

For Mothers

James 5:16

Word Ministries, Inc.

And this is the confidence that we have in him, that, if we ask any thing according to his will, he heareth us: and if we know that he hear us, whatsoever we ask, we know that we have the petitions that we desired of him.

1 John 5:14,15

Harrison House
Tulsa, Oklahoma

9th Printing
Over 76,000 in Print

Prayers That Avail Much
For Mothers
ISBN 0-89274-954-7
Copyright © 1990 by Word Ministries, Inc.
38 Sloan St.
Roswell, GA 30075

Published by Harrison House, Inc.
P. O. Box 35035
Tulsa, Oklahoma 74153

CONTENTS

Part II — What The Word Says

What the Word Says About You

Part III — What Others Say

Part IV — Getting Into the Word

FOREWORD

This very special *Prayers That Avail Much for Mothers* was created and designed for you, because you are important to your family and your Heavenly Father. The unique features in this book will strengthen you spiritually, physically and emotionally and are designed for your daily use as you seek to become a more godly and Spirit-led mother.

Because you face more complex situations and lead a vastly different life than your mother did when she was raising you, the stress of being a mother has also increased. For this reason we have published *Prayers That Avail Much for Mothers,* we want to encourage you with God's Word. Being a godly mother today involves more than raising children and managing a household — it is being the woman and mother that God wants you to become.

We have included different sections within this book to help you in each area of your life. Here is a brief description and a guide to using these sections.

The scriptural prayers in Section I are taken from *Prayers That Avail Much, Volumes I and II,* and

13

are based upon God's Word. More than fifty prayers help you pray more effectively by praying the Scriptures. These prayers were written for specific situations that mothers face and have special meaning for you. Use these scripturally based prayers during your daily quiet time as a solid Bible reference. You will find encouragement and strength in praying God's Word over your life and family.

Section II is devoted completely to the promises that God's Word holds for you as a mother. Appropriately titled "What the Word Says," there are more than five hundred scriptures covering situations and phases of life that are unique to mothers. These scriptures are for you to use as encouragement and guidance as to what the Word of God says about your specific situation. Grouped into two sections, you will read "What the Word Says About You," and "What the Word Says About You and Your Family." The Bible holds promises intended especially for mothers, and you can make these promises a reality in your life by applying these scriptures.

Often, people who have been in your shoes can best encourage and give you hope that it isn't impossible — God does have the answer! Section III, "What Others Say," is full of quotes and insights shared by other women and mothers. These women are all godly examples for you to follow, and are either noted in the ministry themselves or fulfill the valuable role of a leading minister's wife. The truths they share will bolster you and urge you to press forward until you see your troubles turn into victories! You can rely upon this to show you the light at the end of the tunnel.

Section IV, the final section, "Getting Into the Word," gives you step-by-step, practical ways of studying and applying God's Word. To help you develop a consistent and effective prayer life and study time, we have included a 31-Day Devotional and a "Reading the Bible in One Year" program.

The 31-Day Devotional gives you a pattern for successful Bible study and daily encouragement from the Word of God and shows you how you can apply the Word each day. You will learn how to practice what the Bible teaches and grow spiritually because of your diligence in this special time with the Father.

Your "Reading the Bible in One Year" program gives you specific books and chapters of the Bible for you to read each day, including a daily passage from either the Psalms or Proverbs. As you read through the greatest Book of all times, you will be encouraged, nurtured and loved by your Heavenly Father. As you seek to be closer to Him, He will draw closer to you.

What society asks of women is impossible without the help of God and a stable, consistent relationship with Jesus Christ. We have developed this book to encourage and assist you in strength-

15

ening your one-on-one relationship with Him. You, as a mother, affect more than just your family — you are helping shape generations. Such a task is not accomplished successfully without help and love from a close adviser. That is what we want *Prayers That Avail Much for Mothers* to be, a friend in every situation and phase of life. May God bless you!

PREFACE

The prayers in this book are to be used by you for yourself and for others. They are a matter of the heart. Deliberately feed them into your spirit. Allow the Holy Spirit to make the Word a reality in your heart. Your spirit will become quickened to God's Word, and you will begin to think like God thinks and talk like He talks. You will find yourself poring over His Word — hungering for more and more. The Father rewards those who diligently seek Him. (Heb. 11:6)

Meditate upon the Scriptures listed with these prayers. These are by no means the only Scriptures on certain subjects, but they are a beginning.

These prayers are to be a help and a guide to you in order for you to get better acquainted with your heavenly Father and His Word. Not only does His Word affect your life, but also it will affect your family and others through you, for you will be able to counsel accurately those who come to you for advice. If you cannot counsel someone with the Word, you do not have anything with which to counsel. Walk in God's counsel, and prize His wisdom. (Ps. 1; Prov. 4:7,8.) People are looking for something on which they can depend.

When someone in need comes to you, you can point him to that portion in God's Word that is the answer to his problem. You become victorious, trustworthy, and the one with the answer, for your heart is fixed and established on His Word. (Ps. 112.)

Once you begin delving into God's Word, you must commit to ordering your conversation aright. (Ps. 50:23.) That is being a doer of the Word. Faith always has a good report. You cannot pray effectively for yourself, for someone else, or about something and then talk negatively about the matter. (Matt. 12:34-37.) This is being double-minded, and a double-minded man receives *nothing* from God. (James 1:6-8.)

In Ephesians 4:29-30 AMP it is written:

> **Let no foul or polluting language, nor evil word, nor unwholesome or worthless talk [ever] come out of your mouth; but only such [speech] as is good and beneficial to the spiritual progress of others, as is fitting to the need and the occasion, that it may be a blessing and give grace (God's favor) to those who hear it.**

> **And do not grieve the Holy Spirit of God, (do not offend, or vex, or sadden Him) by whom you were sealed (marked, branded as God's own, secured) for the day of redemption — of final deliverance through Christ from evil and the consequences of sin.**

18

Allow these words to sink into your innermost being. Our Father has much, so very much, to say about that little member, the tongue. (James 3.) Give the devil no opportunity by getting into worry, unforgiveness, strife, and criticism. Put a stop to idle and foolish talking. (Eph. 4:27; 5:4.) You are to be a blessing to others. (Gal. 6:10.)

Talk the answer, not the problem. The answer is in God's Word. You must have knowledge of that Word — revelation knowledge. (1 Cor. 2:7-16.)

As an intercessor, unite with others in prayer. United prayer is a mighty weapon that the Body of Christ is to use.

Believe you receive when you pray. Confess the Word. Hold fast to your confession of faith in God's Word. Allow your spirit to pray by the Holy Spirit. Praise God for the victory *now* before any manifestation. *Walk by faith and not by sight.* (2 Cor. 5:7.)

Don't be moved by adverse circumstances. As Satan attempts to challenge you, resist him steadfast in the faith — letting patience have her perfect work. (James 1:4.) Take the Sword of the Spirit and the shield of faith and quench his every fiery dart. (Eph. 6:16,17.) The entire substitutionary work of Christ was for you. Satan is now a defeated foe because Jesus conquered him. (Col. 2:14,15.) Satan is overcome by the blood of the Lamb and the Word of our testimony. (Rev. 12:11.) Fight the good fight of faith. (1 Tim. 6:12.)

Withstand the adversary and be firm in faith against his onset — rooted, established, strong, and determined. (1 Pet. 5:9.) Speak God's Word boldly and courageously.

Your desire should be to please and to bless the Father. As you pray in line with His Word, He joyfully hears that you — His child — are living and walking in the Truth. (3 John 4.)

How exciting to know that the prayers of the saints are forever in the throne room. (Rev. 5:8.) Hallelujah!

Praise God for His Word and the limitlessness of prayer in the name of Jesus. It belongs to every child of God. Therefore, run with patience the race that is set before you, looking unto Jesus the author and finisher of your faith. (Heb. 12:1,2.) God's Word is able to build you up and give you your rightful inheritance among all God's set apart ones. (Acts 20:32.)

Commit yourself to pray and to pray correctly by approaching the throne with your mouth filled with His Word!

INTRODUCTION

> ...The earnest (heart-felt, continued)
> prayer of a righteous man makes tremendous
> power available — dynamic in its working.
>
> James 5:16 AMP

Prayer is fellowshiping with the Father — a
vital, personal contact with God Who is more than
enough. We are to be in constant communion
with Him:

> For the eyes of the Lord are upon the
> righteous — those who are upright and in right
> standing with God — and His ears are attentive
> (open) to their prayer....
>
> 1 Peter 3:12 AMP

Prayer is not to be a religious form with no
power. It is to be effective and accurate and bring
results. God watches over His Word to perform
it. (Jer. 1:12.)

Prayer that brings results must be based on
God's Word.

> For the Word that God speaks is alive and
> full of power — making it active, operative,
> energizing and effective; it is sharper than any
> two-edged sword, penetrating to the dividing
> line of the breath of life (soul) and [the immor-
> tal] spirit, and of joints and marrow [that is,

21

**of the deepest parts of our nature] exposing and
sifting and analyzing and judging the very
thoughts and purposes of the heart.**

Hebrews 4:12 AMP

Prayer is this "living" Word in our mouths.
Our mouths must speak forth faith, for faith is
what pleases God. (Heb. 11:6.) We hold His Word
up to Him in prayer, and our Father sees Himself
in His Word.

God's Word is our contact with Him. We put
Him in remembrance of His Word (Is. 43:26)
placing a demand on His ability in the name of
our Lord Jesus. We remind Him that He supplies
all of our needs according to His riches in glory
by Christ Jesus. (Phil. 4:19.) That Word does not
return to Him void — without producing any
effect, useless — but it *shall* accomplish that which
He pleases and purposes, and it shall prosper in
the thing for which He sent it. (Is. 55:11.)
Hallelujah!

God did *not* leave us without His thoughts and
His ways for we have His Word — His bond. God
instructs us to call Him, and He will answer and
show us great and mighty things. (Jer. 33:3.)
Prayer is to be exciting — not drudgery.

It takes someone to pray. God moves as we
pray in faith — believing. He says that His eyes
run to and fro throughout the whole earth to show
Himself strong in behalf of those whose hearts
are blameless toward Him. (2 Chron. 16:9.)

We are blameless. (Eph. 1:4.) We are His very own children. (Eph. 1:5.) We are His righteousness in Christ Jesus. (2 Cor. 5:21.) He tells us to come boldly to the throne of grace and *obtain* mercy and find grace to help in time of need — appropriate and well-timed help. (Heb. 4:16.) Praise the Lord!

The prayer armor is for every believer, every member of the Body of Christ, who will put it on and walk in it, for the weapons of our warfare are *not carnal* but mighty through God for the pulling down of the strongholds of the enemy (Satan, the god of this world, and all his demonic forces). Spiritual warfare takes place in prayer. (2 Cor. 10:4, Eph. 6:12,18.)

There are many different kinds of prayer, such as the prayer of thanksgiving and praise, the prayer of dedication and worship, and the prayer that changes *things* (not God). All prayer involves time of fellowshiping with the Father.

In Ephesians 6, we are instructed to take the Sword of the Spirit which is the Word of God and **pray at all times — on every occasion, in every season — in the Spirit, with all [manner of] prayer and entreaty** (Eph. 6:18 AMP).

In 1 Timothy 2 we are admonished and urged that **petitions, prayers, intercessions and thanksgivings be offered on behalf of all men** (1 Tim. 2:1 AMP). *Prayer is our responsibility.*

Prayer must be the foundation of every Christian endeavor. Any failure is a prayer failure.

23

We are *not* to be ignorant concerning God's Word. God desires for His people to be successful, to be filled with a full, deep, and clear knowledge of His will (His Word), and to bear fruit in every good work. (Col. 1:9-13.) We then bring honor and glory to Him. (John 15:8.) He desires that we know how to pray for **the prayer of the upright is his delight** (Prov. 15:8).

Our Father has not left us helpless. Not only has He given us His Word, but also He has given us the Holy Spirit to help our infirmities when we know not how to pray as we ought. (Rom. 8:26.) Praise God! Our Father has provided His people with every possible avenue to insure their complete and total victory in this life in the name of our Lord Jesus. (1 John 5:3-5.)

We pray to the Father, in the name of Jesus, through the Holy Spirit, according to the Word!

Using God's Word on purpose, specifically, in prayer is one means of prayer, and it is a most effective and accurate means. Jesus said, **The words (truths) that I have been speaking to you are spirit and life** (John 6:63 AMP).

When Jesus faced Satan in the wilderness, He said, ''It is written. . .it is written. . .it is written.'' We are to live, be upheld, and sustained by every Word that proceeds from the mouth of God. (Matt. 4:4.)

James, by the Spirit, admonishes that we do not have, because we do not ask. We ask and receive not, because we ask amiss. (James 4:2,3.) We must heed that admonishment now for we are to become experts in prayer rightly dividing the Word of Truth. (2 Tim. 2:15.)

Using the Word in prayer is *not* taking it out of context, for His Word in us is the key to answered prayer — to prayer that brings results. He is able to do exceedingly abundantly above all we ask or think, according to the power that works in us. (Eph. 3:20.) The power lies within God's Word. It is anointed by the Holy Spirit. The Spirit of God does not lead us apart from the Word, for the Word is of the Spirit of God. We apply that Word personally to ourselves and to others — not adding to or taking from it — in the name of Jesus. We apply the Word to the *now* — to those things, circumstances, and situations facing each of us *now*.

Paul was very specific and definite in his praying. The first chapters of Ephesians, Philippians, Colossians, and 2 Thessalonians are examples of how Paul prayed for believers. There are numerous others. *Search them out.* Paul wrote under the inspiration of the Holy Spirit. We can use these Spirit-given prayers today!

In 2 Corinthians 1:11, 2 Corinthians 9:14, and Philippians 1:4, we see examples of how believers prayed one for another — putting others first in their prayer life with *joy.* Our faith does work by love. (Gal. 5:6.) We grow spiritually as we reach out to help others — praying for and with them and holding out to them the Word of Life. (Phil. 2:16.)

Man is a spirit, he has a soul, and he lives in a body. (1 Thess. 5:23.) In order to operate successfully, each of these three parts must be fed properly. The soul or intellect feeds on intellectual food to produce intellectual strength. The body feeds on physical food to produce physical strength. The spirit — the heart or inward man — is the real you, the part that has been reborn in Christ Jesus. It must feed on spirit food which is God's Word in order to produce and develop faith. As we feast upon God's Word, our minds become renewed with His Word, and we have a fresh mental and spiritual attitude. (Eph. 4:23,24.)

Likewise, we are to present our bodies a living sacrifice, holy, acceptable unto God (Rom. 12:1) and not let that body dominate us but bring it into subjection to the spirit man. (1 Cor. 9:27.) God's Word is healing and health to all our flesh. (Prov. 4:22.) Therefore, God's Word affects each part of us — spirit, soul and body. We become vitally united to the Father, to Jesus, and to the Holy Spirit — one with Them. (John 16:13-15, John 17:21, Col. 2:10.)

God's Word, this spirit food, takes root in our hearts, is formed by the tongue, and is spoken out of our mouths. This is creative power. The spoken Word works as we confess it and then apply the action to it.

Be doers of the Word, and not hearers only, deceiving your own selves. (James 1:22.) Faith without works or corresponding action is *dead*. (James 2:17.) Don't be mental assenters — those who agree that the Bible is true but never act on it. *Real faith is acting on God's Word now*. We cannot build faith without practicing the Word. We cannot develop an effective prayer life that is anything but empty words unless God's Word actually has a part in our lives. We are to hold fast to our *confession* of the Word's truthfulness. Our Lord Jesus is the High Priest of our confession (Heb. 3:1), and He is the Guarantee of a better agreement — a more excellent and advantageous covenant. (Heb. 7:22.)

Prayer does not cause faith to work, but faith causes prayer to work. Therefore, any prayer problem is a problem of doubt — doubting the integrity of the Word and the ability of God to stand behind His promises or the statements of fact in the Word.

We can spend fruitless hours in prayer if our hearts are not prepared beforehand. Preparation of the heart, the spirit, comes from meditation in the Father's Word, meditation on what we are in Christ, what He is to us, and what the Holy Spirit can mean to us as we become God-inside minded. As God told Joshua (Josh. 1:8), as we

27

meditate on the Word day and night, and do according to all that is written, then shall we make our way prosperous and have good success. We are to attend to God's Word, submit to His sayings, keep them in the center of our hearts, and put away contrary talk. (Prov. 4:20-24.)

When we use God's Word in prayer, this is *not* something we just rush through uttering once, and we are finished. Do *not* be mistaken. There is nothing "magical" nor "manipulative" about it — no set pattern or device in order to satisfy what we want or think out of our flesh. Instead we are holding God's Word before Him. We confess what He says belongs to us.

We expect His divine intervention while we choose not to look at the things that are seen but at the things that are unseen, for the things that are seen are subject to change. (2 Cor. 4:18.)

Prayer based upon the Word rises above the senses, contacts the Author of the Word and sets His spiritual laws into motion. Is it not just saying prayers that gets results, but it is spending time with the Father, learning His wisdom, drawing on His strength, being filled with His quietness, and basking in His love that bring results to our prayers. Praise the Lord!

*   *   *

The prayers in this book are designed to teach and train you in the art of personal confession and intercessory prayer. As you pray them, you will be reinforcing the prayer armor which we have been instructed to put on in Ephesians 6:11. The fabric from which the armor is made is the Word of God. We are to live by every word that proceeds from the mouth of God.

We desire the whole counsel of God, because we know it changes us. By receiving that counsel, you will be . . . **transformed (changed) by the [entire] renewal of your mind — by its new ideals and attitude — so that you may prove [for yourselves] what is the good and acceptable and perfect will of God, even the thing which is good and acceptable and perfect [in His sight for you]** (Rom. 12:2 AMP).

The prayers of personal confession of the Word of God for yourself can also be used as intercessory prayers for others by simply praying them in the third person, changing the pronouns *I* or *we* to the name of the person or persons for whom you are interceding and adjusting the verbs accordingly.

The prayers of intercession have blanks in which you are to fill in the spaces with the name of the person(s) for whom you are praying. These prayers of intercession can likewise be made into prayers of personal confession for yourself by inserting your own name and the proper personal pronoun in the appropriate places.

An often-asked question is: "How many times should I pray the same prayer?"

The answer is simple: you pray until you know that the answer is fixed in your heart. After that, you need to repeat the prayer whenever adverse circumstances or long delays cause you to be tempted to doubt that your prayer has been heard and your request granted.

The Word of God is your weapon against the temptation to lose heart and grow weary in your prayer life. When that Word of promise becomes fixed in your heart, you will find yourself praising, giving glory to God for the answer, even when the only evidence you have of that answer is your own faith.

Another question often asked is: "When we repeat prayers more than once, aren't we praying 'vain repetitions'?"

Obviously, such people are referring to the admonition of Jesus when He told His disciples: **And when you pray do not (multiply words, repeating the same ones over and over, and) heap up phrases as the Gentiles do, for they think they will be heard for their much speaking** (Matt. 6:7 AMP). Praying the Word of God is not praying the kind of prayer that the "heathen" pray. You will note in 1 Kings 18:25-29 the manner of prayer that was offered to the gods who could not hear. That is not the way you and I pray. The words that we speak are not vain, but they are spirit and life, and mighty through God to the pulling down of strongholds. We have a God Whose eyes are over the righteous and Whose ears are open to us: when we pray, He hears us.

You are the righteousness of God in Christ Jesus, and your prayers will avail much. They will bring salvation to the sinner, deliverance to the oppressed, healing to the sick, and prosperity to the poor. They will usher in the next move of God in the earth. In addition to affecting outward circumstances and other people, your prayers will also have an effect upon you. In the very process of praying, your life will be changed as you go from faith to faith and from glory to glory.

As a Christian, your first priority is to love the Lord your God with your entire being, and your neighbor as yourself. You are called to be an intercessor, a man or woman of prayer. You are to seek the face of the Lord as you inquire, listen, meditate and consider in the temple of the Lord.

As one of "God's set-apart ones," the will of the Lord for your life is the same as it is for the life of every other true believer: **. . . seek ye first the kingdom of God, and his righteousness; and all these things shall be added unto you** (Matt. 6:33).

Personal Confessions

Jesus is Lord over my spirit, my soul, and my body. (Phil. 2:9-11.)

Jesus has been made unto me wisdom, righteousness, sanctification, and redemption. I can do all things through Christ Who strengthens me. (1 Cor. 1:30, Phil. 4:13.)

The Lord is my shepherd. I do not want. My God supplies all my need according to His riches in glory in Christ Jesus. (Ps. 23, Phil. 4:19.)

I do not fret or have anxiety about anything. I do not have a care. (Phil. 4:6, 1 Pet. 5:6,7.)

I am the Body of Christ. I am redeemed from the curse, because Jesus bore my sicknesses and carried my diseases in His own body. By His stripes I am healed. I forbid any sickness or disease to operate in my body. Every organ, every tissue of my body functions in the perfection in which God created it to function. I honor God and bring glory to Him in my body. (Gal. 3:13, Matt. 8:17, 1 Pet. 2:24, 1 Cor. 6:20.)

I have the mind of Christ and hold the thoughts, feelings, and purposes of His heart. (1 Cor. 2:16.)

I am a believer and not a doubter. I hold fast to my confession of faith. I decide to walk by faith and practice faith. My faith comes by hearing and hearing by the Word of God. Jesus is the author and the developer of my faith. (Heb. 4:14, Heb. 11:6, Rom. 10:17, Heb. 12:2.)

The love of God has been shed abroad in my heart by the Holy Spirit and His love abides in me richly. I keep myself in the Kingdom of light, in love, in the Word, and the wicked one touches me not. (Rom. 5:5, 1 John 4:16, 1 John 5:18.)

I tread upon serpents and scorpions and over all the power of the enemy. I take my shield of faith and quench his every fiery dart. Greater is He Who is in me than he who is in the world. (Ps. 91:13, Eph. 6:16, 1 John 4:4.)

I am delivered from this present evil world. I am seated with Christ in heavenly places. I reside in the Kingdom of God's dear Son. The law of the Spirit of life in Christ Jesus has made me free from the law of sin and death. (Gal. 1:4, Eph. 2:6, Col. 1:13, Rom. 8:2.)

I fear *not* for God has given me a spirit of power, of love, and of a sound mind. God is on my side. (2 Tim. 1:7, Rom. 8:31.)

I hear the voice of the Good Shepherd. I hear my Father's voice, and the voice of a stranger I will not follow. I roll my works upon the Lord. I commit and trust them wholly to Him. He will cause my thoughts to become agreeable to His will, and so shall my plans be established and succeed. (John 10:27, Prov. 16:3.)

I am a world overcomer because I am born of God. I represent the Father and Jesus well. I am a useful member in the Body of Christ. I am His workmanship recreated in Christ Jesus. My Father God is all the while effectually at work in me both to will and do His good pleasure. (1 John 5:4-5, Eph. 2:10, Phil. 2:13.)

I let the Word dwell in me richly. He Who began a good work in me will continue until the day of Christ. (Col. 3:16, Phil. 1:6.)

Part I
Prayers That Avail Much

1

To WALK IN THE WORD

Father, in the name of Jesus, *I commit myself to walk in the Word.* Your Word living in me produces Your life in this world. I recognize that Your Word is integrity itself — steadfast, sure, eternal — and I trust my life to its provisions.

You have sent your Word forth into my heart. I let it dwell in me richly in all wisdom. I meditate in it day and night so that I may diligently act on it. The Incorruptible Seed, the Living Word, the Word of Truth, is abiding in my spirit. That Seed is growing mightily in me now, producing Your nature, Your life. It is my counsel, my shield, my buckler, my powerful weapon in battle. The Word is a lamp to my feet and a light to my path. It makes my way plain before me. I do not stumble, for my steps are ordered in the Word.

The Holy Spirit leads and guides me into all the truth. He gives me understanding, discernment, and comprehension so that I am preserved from the snares of the evil one.

I delight myself in You and Your Word. Because of that, You put Your desires within my heart. I commit my way unto You, and You bring it to pass. I am confident that You are at work in me now both to will and to do all Your good pleasure.

I exalt Your Word, hold it in high esteem, and give it first place. *I make my schedule around Your Word.* I make the Word final authority to settle all questions that confront me. I choose to agree with the Word of God, and I choose to disagree with any thoughts, conditions, or circumstances contrary to Your Word. I boldly and confidently say that my heart is fixed and established on the solid foundation — the living Word of God!

Scripture References

Hebrews 4:12	1 Peter 3:12
Colossians 3:16	Colossians 4:2
Joshua 1:8	Ephesians 6:10
1 Peter 1:23	Luke 18:1
Psalm 91:4	James 5:16
Psalm 119:105	Psalm 37:4,5
Psalm 37:23	Philippians 2:13
Colossians 1:9	2 Corinthians 10:5
John 16:13	Psalm 112:7,8

2
To pray

Father, in the name of Jesus, I offer up thanksgiving that You have called me to be a fellow workman — a joint promoter and a laborer together — with and for You. I commit myself to pray and not to turn coward — faint, lose heart, or give up.

Fearlessly and confidently and boldly I draw near to the throne of grace that I may receive mercy and find grace to help in good time for every need — appropriate help and well-timed help, coming just when I (and others) need it. This is the confidence that I have in You, that, if I ask anything according to Your will, You hear me: and if I know that You hear me, whatsoever I ask, I know that I have the petitions that I desired of You.

When I do not know what prayer to offer and how to offer it worthily as I ought, I thank You, Father, that the (Holy) Spirit comes to my aid and bears me up in my weakness (my inability to produce results). He, the Holy Spirit, goes to meet my supplication and pleads in my behalf

39

with unspeakable yearnings and groanings too deep for utterance. And He Who searches the hearts of men knows what is in the mind of the (Holy) Spirit. The Holy Spirit intercedes and pleads in behalf of the saints according to and in harmony with God's will. Therefore, I am assured and know that (God being a partner in my labor) all things work together and are [fitting into a plan] for my good, because I love God and am called according to [His] design and purpose.

I do not fret or have any anxiety about anything, but in every circumstance and in everything by prayer and petition [definite requests] with thanksgiving continue to make my wants (and the wants of others) known to God. Whatever I ask for in prayer, I believe that it is granted to me, and I will receive it.

The earnest (heartfelt, continued) prayer of a righteous man makes tremendous power available — dynamic in its working. Father, I live in You — abide vitally united to You — and Your words remain in me and continue to live in my heart. Therefore I ask whatever I will and it shall be done for me. When I bear (produce) much fruit (through prayer), You, Father, are honored and glorified. Hallelujah!

Scripture References

1 Corinthians 3:9 AMP
Luke 18:1 AMP
Hebrews 4:16 AMP
1 John 5:14,15
Romans 8:26-29 AMP

Philippians 4:6 AMP
Mark 11:24 AMP
James 5:16b AMP
John 15:7,8 AMP

3
To PUT ON THE
ARMOR OF GOD

In the name of Jesus, I put on the whole armor of God, that I may be able to stand against the wiles of the devil, for I wrestle not against flesh and blood, but against principalities, powers, the rulers of the darkness of this world, and against spiritual wickedness in high places.

Therefore, I take unto myself the whole armor of God, that I may be able to withstand in the evil day, and having done all, to stand. I stand, therefore, having my loins girt about with truth. Your Word, Lord, which is truth, contains all the weapons of my warfare which are not carnal, but mighty through God to the pulling down of strongholds.

I have on the breastplate of righteousness; which is faith and love. My feet are shod with the preparation of the Gospel of peace. In Christ Jesus I have peace, and pursue peace with all men. I am a minister of reconciliation proclaiming the good news of the Gospel.

I take the shield of faith, wherewith I am able to quench all the fiery darts of the wicked, the helmet of salvation *(holding the thoughts, feelings, and purpose of God's heart)* and the sword of the Spirit, which is the Word of God. In the face of all trials, tests, temptations and tribulation, I cut to pieces the snare of the enemy by speaking the Word of God. Greater is He that is in me than he that is in the world.

Thank You, Father, for the armor. I will pray at all times — on every occasion, in every season — in the Spirit, with all [manner of] prayer and entreaty. To that end I will keep alert and watch with strong purpose and perseverance, interceding in behalf of all the saints. My power and ability and sufficiency are from God Who has qualified me as a minister and a dispenser of a new covenant [of salvation through Christ]. Amen.

Scripture References

Ephesians 6:11-14a

John 17:17b

2 Corinthians 10:4

Ephesians 6:14b,15 AMP

Ephesians 2:14

Psalm 34:14

2 Corinthians 5:18

Ephesians 6:16,17 AMP

1 John 4:4b

2 Corinthians 3:5,6 AMP

4

To GLORIFY GOD

In view of [all] the mercies of God, I make a decisive dedication of my body — presenting all my members and faculties — as a living sacrifice, holy (devoted, consecrated) and well pleasing to You, God, which is my reasonable (rational, intelligent) service and spiritual worship. It is [not in my own strength] for it is You, Lord, Who is all the while effectually at work in me — energizing and creating in me the power and desire — both to will and work for Your good pleasure and satisfaction and delight.

Father, I will not draw back or shrink in fear, for then Your soul would have no delight or pleasure in me. I was bought for a price — purchased with a preciousness and paid for, made Your very own. So, then, I honor You, Lord, and bring glory to You in my body.

I called on You in the day of trouble; You delivered me, and I shall honor and glorify you. I rejoice because You delivered me and drew me to Yourself out of the control and dominion of darkness (*obscurity*) and transferred me into the kingdom of the Son of Your love. I will confess and praise You, O Lord my God, with my whole (united) heart; and I will glorify Your name for evermore.

As a bond servant of Jesus Christ, I receive and develop the talents which have been given me, for I would have You say of me, ''Well done, you upright (honorable, admirable) and faithful servant!'' I make use of the gifts (faculties, talents, qualities) according to the grace given me. I let my light so shine before men that they may see my moral excellence and my praiseworthy, noble and good deeds, and recognize and honor and praise and glorify my Father Who is in heaven.

In the name of Jesus, I allow my life to lovingly express truth in all things — speaking truly, dealing truly, living truly. Whatever I do — no matter what it is — in word or deed, I do everything in the name of the Lord Jesus and in [dependence upon] His Person, giving praise to God the Father through Him. Whatever may be my task, I work at it heartily (from the soul), as [something done] for the Lord and not for men. To God the Father be all glory and honor and praise. Amen.

Scripture References (AMP)

Romans 12:1	Matthew 25:21
Philippians 2:13	Romans 12:6
Hebrews 10:38b	Matthew 5:16
1 Corinthians 6:20	Ephesians 4:15
Psalm 50:15	Colossians 3:17
Colossians 1:13	Colossians 3:23
Psalm 86:12	

5

To BE GOD-INSIDE MINDED

I am a spirit, I have a soul, and I live in a physical body. My spirit is the candle of the Lord. God, my Father, is guiding me into all the truth through my spirit.

I am a child of God, born of the Spirit of God, filled with the Spirit of God, and led by the Spirit of God. I listen to my heart as I look to my spirit inside me.

The Holy Spirit gives direction to my spirit and illumination to my mind. He leads me in the way I should go in all the affairs of life. He leads me by an inward witness. The eyes of my understanding are being enlightened. Wisdom is in my inward parts. His love is perfected in me. I have an unction from the Holy One.

I am becoming spirit-conscious. I listen to the voice of my spirit and obey what my spirit tells me. I let my spirit dominate me, for I walk not after the flesh, but after the spirit. I examine my leading in the light of His Word. I trust in the Lord with all my heart and lean not to my own understanding. In all my ways I acknowledge Him, and He directs my paths. I walk in the light of God's Word.

I will educate and train and develop my human spirit. The Word of God shall not depart out of my mouth. I meditate therein day and night. Therefore I shall make my way prosperous, and I will have good success in life. *I am a doer of the Word and put God's Word first.* My spirit man is in the ascendancy.

Thanks be unto God who always causes me to triumph in Christ!

Scripture References

1 Thessalonians 5:23	Job 38:36
Proverbs 20:27	1 John 4:12
John 16:13	1 John 2:20
Romans 8:14,16	Romans 9:1
John 3:6,7	Romans 8:1
John 7:37-39	Proverbs 3:5,6
Ephesians 5:18	Psalm 119:105
Isaiah 48:17	Joshua 1:8
Ephesians 1:18	James 1:22
1 Corinthians 1:30	2 Corinthians 2:14

6

To REJOICE IN THE LORD

Father, this is the day the Lord has made. I rejoice and I am glad in it! I rejoice in you always. And again I say, I rejoice. I delight myself in You, Lord. Happy am I because God is my Lord!

Father, You say that You rejoice over me with joy. Hallelujah! I am redeemed. I come with singing, and everlasting joy is upon my head. I obtain joy and gladness, and sorrow and sighing flee away. That spirit of rejoicing, joy, and laughter is my heritage. Where the Spirit of the Lord is there is liberty — emancipation from bondage, freedom. I walk in that liberty.

Father, my mouth shall praise You with joyful lips. I am ever filled and stimulated with the Holy Spirit. I speak out in psalms and hymns and make melody with all my heart to You, Lord. My happy heart is a good medicine and my cheerful mind works healing. The light in my eyes rejoices the heart of others. I have a good report. My countenance radiates the joy of the Lord.

Father, I thank You that I bear much prayer fruit. I ask in Jesus' name, and I will receive so that my joy (gladness, delight) may be full, complete, and overflowing. That joy of the Lord is my *strength*. Therefore, I can count it all joy, all strength, when I encounter tests or trials of any sort because I am strong in You, Father.

I have the *victory* in the name of Jesus. Satan is under my feet. I am not moved by adverse circumstances. I have been made the righteousness of God in Christ Jesus. I dwell in the Kingdom of God and have peace and joy in the Holy Spirit! Praise the Lord!

Scripture References

Psalm 118:24	Philippians 4:8
Philippians 4:4	Proverbs 15:13
Philippians 3:1	John 15:7,8
Psalm 144:15	John 16:23
Zephaniah 3:17	Nehemiah 8:10
Isaiah 51:11	James 1:2
2 Corinthians 3:17	Ephesians 6:10
James 1:25	1 John 5:4
Psalm 63:5	Ephesians 1:22
Ephesians 5:18,19	2 Corinthians 5:7
Proverbs 17:22	2 Corinthians 5:21
Proverbs 15:30	Romans 14:17

7

To WALK IN GOD'S WISDOM AND HIS PERFECT WILL

Father, I thank you that the communication of my faith becomes effectual by acknowledging every good thing which is in me in Christ Jesus. I hear the voice of the Good Shepherd. I hear my Father's voice, and the voice of a stranger I will not follow.

Father, I believe in my heart and say with my mouth that *this day the will of God is done in my life.* I walk in a manner worthy of You Lord, fully pleasing to You and desiring to please You in all things, bearing fruit in every good work. Jesus has been made unto me wisdom. I single-mindedly walk in that wisdom expecting to know what to do in every situation and to be on *top* of every circumstance!

I roll my works upon You, Lord, and You make my thoughts agreeable to Your will, and so my plans are established and succeed. You direct my steps and make them sure. I understand and firmly grasp what the will of the Lord is for I am not vague, thoughtless, or foolish. I stand firm and mature in spiritual growth, convinced and fully assured in everything willed by God.

Father, You have destined and appointed me to come progressively to know Your will — that is to perceive, to recognize more strongly and clearly, and to become better and more intimately acquainted with Your will. I thank you, Father, for the Holy Spirit Who abides permanently in me and Who guides me into all the truth — the whole, full truth — and speaks whatever He hears from the Father and announces and declares to me the things that are to come. I have the mind of Christ and hold the thoughts, feelings, and purposes of His heart.

So, Father, I have entered into that blessed rest by adhering, trusting, and relying on You in the name of Jesus. Hallelujah!

Scripture References

Philemon 6
John 10:27
John 10:5
Colossians 1:9,10 AMP
1 Corinthians 1:30
James 1:5-8
Proverbs 16:3,9 AMP

Ephesians 5:17
Colossians 4:12 AMP
Acts 22:14
1 John 2:20,27
1 Corinthians 2:16
Hebrews 4:10
John 16:13 AMP

8

To SANCTIFICATION

Father, in the name of Jesus, I commit myself to a sanctified life — a life of holiness, pleasing to You.

Your Word says to wash ourselves and make ourselves clean, to cease to do evil and learn to do well. Therefore, Father, I repent and turn from any sin in my life and wash myself with the water of the Word. I cleanse myself from all filthiness of the flesh and spirit, perfecting holiness in fear and reverence of You, Lord.

Father, I receive Your forgiveness now and thank You for it, because Your Word says You are faithful and just to forgive us our sins and to cleanse us from all unrighteousness. Thank You that Jesus has been made unto me wisdom, righteousness, sanctification, and redemption. Lord Jesus, You sanctify me through Your truth: Your Word is truth.

I submit myself to You, Lord — spirit, soul, and body. I commit to change whatever needs to be changed in my life, because the desire of my heart is to be a vessel unto honor, sanctified, and fitting for the Master's use and prepared for every good work.

Thank You, Lord, that I eat the good of the land, because I am willing and obedient.

Scripture References

Isaiah 1:16,17	1 Corinthians 1:30
Ephesians 5:26	John 17:17
2 Corinthians 7:1	2 Timothy 2:21
1 John 1:8,9	Isaiah 1:19

9

To BEAR FRUIT

Lord Jesus, You said in John 15:16 that You have chosen us and ordained us that we should go and bring forth fruit and that our fruit should remain, that whatsoever we shall ask of the Father in Your name, He may give it to us.

The Apostle Paul said to be filled with the fruit of righteousness and that he desired that fruit might abound to our account. Therefore, I commit myself to bring forth the fruit of the spirit: love, joy, peace, longsuffering, gentleness, goodness, faith, meekness, and temperance.

I renounce and turn from the fruit of the flesh, because I am Christ's and have crucified the flesh with its affections and lusts.

A seed cannot bear fruit unless it first falls into the ground and dies. I confess that I am crucified with Christ: nevertheless I live; yet not I but Christ lives in me. And the life that I now live in the flesh I live by the faith of the Son of God, Who loved me and gave Himself for me.

Father, I thank you that I am good ground, that I hear Your Word and understand it, and that the Word bears fruit in my life — sometimes a hundredfold, sometimes sixty, sometimes thirty. I am like a tree planted by the rivers of water that brings forth fruit in its season. My leaf shall not wither, and whatever I do shall prosper.

Father, thank You for filling me with the knowledge of Your will in all wisdom and spiritual understanding, that I may walk worthy of You, Lord, being fruitful in every good work and increasing in the knowledge of You.

Scripture References

John 15:16

Philippians 1:11

Philippians 4:17

Galatians 5:22-24

John 12:24

Galatians 2:20

Matthew 13:23

Psalm 1:3

Colossians 1:9,10

10
To HELP OTHERS

Father, in the name of Jesus, I will do unto others as I would have them do unto me. I eagerly pursue and seek to acquire [this] *(agape)* love — I make it my aim, my great quest in life.

Father, in the name of Jesus, I will esteem and look upon and be concerned for not [merely] my own interest, but also for the interest of others as they pursue success. I am strong in the Lord, and in the power of His might. I will, on purpose, in the name of Jesus, make it a practice to please (make happy) my neighbor, *(boss, co-worker, teacher, parent, child, brother, etc.)* for his good and for his true welfare, to edify him — that is, to strengthen him and build him up in all ways — spiritually, socially and materially.

Father, in the name of Jesus, I will therefore encourage (admonish, exhort) others and edify — strengthen and build up — others.

Father, in the name of Jesus, I love my enemies *(as well as my business associates, fellow church members, neighbors, those in authority over me)* and am kind and do good — doing favors so that someone derives benefit from them. I lend expecting and hoping for nothing in return, but considering nothing as lost and despairing of no one. Then my recompense (my reward) will be great — rich, strong, intense, and abundant — and I will be a son of the Most High; for He is kind and charitable and good to the ungrateful and selfish and wicked. I am merciful — sympathetic, tender, responsive, and compassionate — even as my Father is [all these]. I am an imitator of God, my Father — therefore, I walk in love.

Thank You, Father, for imprinting Your laws upon my heart, and inscribing them on my mind — on my inmost thoughts and understanding. According to Your Word, as I would like and desire that men would do to me, I do exactly so to them, in the name of Jesus.

Scripture References

Luke 6:31
1 Corinthians 14:1 AMP
Philippians 2:4 AMP
Ephesians 6:10
Romans 15:2 AMP

1 Thessalonians 5:11 AMP
Luke 6:35,36 AMP
Ephesians 5:1,2 AMP
Hebrews 10:16b AMP
Luke 6:31 AMP

11

To WALK IN LOVE

Father, in Jesus' name, I thank You that the love of God has been poured forth into my heart by the Holy Spirit Who has been given to me. I keep and treasure Your Word. The love of and for You, Father, has been perfected and completed in me, and perfect love casts out all fear.

Father, I am Your child, and *I commit to walk in the God kind of love.* I endure long, am patient, and kind. I am never envious and never boil over with jealousy. I am not boastful or vainglorious, and I do not display myself haughtily. I am not rude and unmannerly and I do not act unbecomingly. I do not insist on my own rights or my own way for I am not self-seeking, touchy, fretful or resentful.

I take no account of an evil done to me and pay no attention to a suffered wrong. I do not rejoice at injustice and unrighteousness, but I rejoice when right and truth prevail. I bear up under anything and everything that comes. I am ever ready to believe the *best* of others. My hopes are fadeless under all circumstances. I endure

58

everything without weakening because my love never fails.

Father, I *bless* and *pray* for those who persecute me — who are cruel in their attitude toward me. I bless them and do not curse them. Therefore, my love abounds yet more and more in knowledge and in all judgment. I approve things that are excellent. I am sincere and *without offense* till the day of Christ. I am filled with the fruits of righteousness.

Everywhere I go I commit to plant seeds of love. I thank You, Father, for preparing hearts ahead of time to receive this love. I know that these seeds will produce Your love in the hearts to whom they are given.

Father, I thank You that as I flow in Your love and wisdom, people are being blessed by my life and ministry. Father, You make me to find favor, compassion, and loving) kindness with others (*name them*).

I am rooted deep in love and founded securely on love knowing that You are on my side, and nothing is able to separate me from Your love, Father, which is in Christ Jesus my Lord. Thank you, Father, in Jesus' precious name. Amen.

Scripture References

Romans 5:5

1 John 2:5

1 John 4:18

1 Corinthians 13:4-8 AMP

Romans 12:14 AMP

Matthew 5:44

Philippians 1:9-11

John 13:34

1 Corinthians 3:6

Daniel 1:9 AMP

Ephesians 3:17 AMP

Romans 8:31,39

12

To WALK IN FORGIVENESS

Father, in the name of Jesus, I make a fresh commitment to You to live in peace and harmony, not only with the other brothers and sisters of the Body of Christ, but also with my friends, associates, neighbors, and family.

I let go of all bitterness, resentment, envying, strife, and unkindness in any form. I give no place to the devil in Jesus' name. Now Father, I ask for Your forgiveness. By faith, I receive it, having assurance that I am cleansed from all unrighteousness through Jesus Christ. I ask You to forgive and release all who have wronged and hurt me. I forgive and release them. Deal with them in your mercy and loving-kindness.

From this moment on, I purpose to walk in love, to seek peace, to live in agreement, and to conduct myself toward others in a manner that is pleasing to You. I know that I have right standing with you and Your ears are attentive to my prayers.

It is written in Your Word that the love of God has been poured forth into my heart by the Holy Ghost who is given to me. I believe that love flows forth into the lives of everyone I know, that I may be filled with and abound in the fruits of righteousness which bring glory and honor unto You, Lord, in Jesus' name. So be it!

Scripture References

Romans 12:16-18	Mark 11:25
Romans 12:10	Ephesians 4:32
Philippians 2:2	1 Peter 3:8,11,12
Ephesians 4:31	Colossians 1:10
Ephesians 4:27	Romans 5:5
John 1:9	Philippians 1:11 AMP

13

To WATCH WHAT YOU SAY

Father, today, I make a commitment to You in the name of Jesus. I turn from idle words and foolishly talking things that are contrary to my true desire to myself and toward others. Your Word says that the tongue defiles; that the tongue sets on fire the course of nature; that the tongue is set on fire of hell.

In the name of Jesus, I am determined to take control of my tongue. I am determined that hell will not set my tongue on fire. I renounce, reject, and repent of every word that has ever proceeded out of my mouth against You God and Your operation. I cancel its power and dedicate my mouth to speak excellent and right things. My mouth shall utter truth.

I am the righteousness of God. I set the course of my life for obedience, for abundance, for wisdom, for health, and for joy. Everything I speak is becoming to God. I refuse to compromise or err from pure and sound words. The words of my mouth and my deeds shall show forth Your righteousness and Your salvation all of my days.

I guard my mouth and my heart with all diligence. I refuse to give Satan any place in me.

Father, Your Words are top priority to me. They are spirit and life. I let the Word dwell in me richly in all wisdom. The ability of God is released within me by the words of my mouth and by the Word of God. I speak Your Words out of my mouth. They are alive in me. You are alive and working in me. So, I can boldly say that my words are words of faith, words of power, words of love, and words of life. They produce good things in my life and in the lives of others. Because I choose Your Words for my lips, I choose Your will for my life, and I go forth in the power of those words to perform them in Jesus' name.

Scripture References

Ephesians 5:4

2 Timothy 2:16

James 3:6

Proverbs 8:6,7

2 Corinthians 5:21

Proverbs 4:23

Proverbs 21:23

Ephesians 4:27

James 1:6

John 6:63

Colossians 3:16

Philemon 6

14

To LIVE FREE FROM WORRY

Father, I thank You that I have been delivered from the power of darkness and translated into the Kingdom of Your dear Son. *I commit to live free from worry in the name of Jesus*, for the law of the Spirit of life in Christ Jesus has made me *free* from the law of sin and death.

I humble myself under Your mighty hand that in due time You may exalt me. I cast the whole of my cares (*name them*) — all my anxieties, all my worries, all my concerns, once and for all — on You. You care for me affectionately and care about me watchfully. You sustain me. You will never allow the consistently righteous to be moved — made to slip, fall, or fail!

Father, I delight myself in You, and You perfect that which concerns me.

I cast down imaginations (reasonings) and every high thing that exalts itself against the knowledge of You, and bring into captivity every thought to the obedience of Christ. I lay aside every weight and the sin of worry which does try so easily to beset me. I run with patience the race that is set before me, looking unto Jesus, the author and finisher of my faith.

I thank You, Father, that You are able to keep that which I have committed unto You. I think on (fix my mind on) those things that are true, honest, just, pure, lovely, of good report, virtuous, and deserving of praise. I let not my heart be troubled. I abide in Your Words, and Your Words abide in me. Therefore, Father, I do *not* forget what manner of person I am. I look into the perfect law of liberty and continue therein, being *not* a forgetful hearer, but a *doer of the Word* and thus blessed in my doing!

Thank You, Father. *I am carefree.* I walk in that peace which passes all understanding in Jesus' name!

Scripture References

Colossians 1:13	Hebrews 12:1,2
Romans 8:2	2 Timothy 1:12
1 Peter 5:6,7 AMP	Philippians 4:8
Psalm 55:22	John 14:1
Psalm 37:4,5	John 15:7
Psalm 138:8	James 1:22-25
2 Corinthians 10:5	Philippians 4:6

15

To RECEIVE JESUS
AS SAVIOR AND LORD

Father, it is written in Your Word that if I confess with my mouth that Jesus is Lord and believe in my heart that You have raised Him from the dead, I shall be saved. Therefore, Father, I confess that Jesus is my Lord. I make Him Lord of my life right now. I believe in my heart that You raised Jesus from the dead. I renounce my past life with Satan and close the door to any of his devices.

I thank You for forgiving me of all my sin. Jesus is my Lord, and I am a new creation. Old things have passed away. Now all things become new in Jesus' name. Amen.

Scripture References

John 3:16	John 14:6
John 6:37	Romans 10:9,10
John 10:10b	Romans 10:13
Romans 3:23	Ephesians 2:1-10
2 Corinthians 5:19	2 Corinthians 5:17
John 16:8,9	John 1:12
Romans 5:8	2 Corinthians 5:21

16

To receive the infilling of the holy spirit

My heavenly Father, I am Your child, for I believe in my heart that Jesus has been raised from the dead, and I have confessed Him as my Lord.

Jesus said, "How much more shall your heavenly Father give the Holy Spirit to those who ask Him." I ask You now in the name of Jesus to fill me with the Holy Spirit. I step into the fullness and power that I desire in the name of Jesus.

Scripture References

John 14:16,17   Acts 10:44-46
Luke 11:13   Acts 19:2,5,6
Acts 1:8a   1 Corinthians 14:2-15
Acts 2:4   1 Corinthians 14:18,27
Acts 2:32,33,39   Ephesians 6:18
Acts 8:12-17   Jude 1:20

17

ADORATION
"Hallowed Be Thy Name"

Our Father, which art in heaven, hallowed be Thy name.

Bless the Lord, O my soul: and all that is within me, bless Your Holy name. I adore You and make known to You my adoration and love this day.

I bless Your name, *Elohim*, the Creator of heaven and earth, Who was in the beginning. It is You Who made me, and You have crowned me with glory and honor. You are the God of might and strength. Hallowed be Thy name!

I bless Your name, *El-Shaddai*, the God Almighty of Blessings. You are the Breasty One Who nourishes and supplies. You are All-Bountiful and All-Sufficient. Hallowed be Thy name!

I bless Your name, *Adonai*, my Lord and my Master. You are Jehovah — the Completely Self-Existing One, always present, revealed in Jesus

69

Who is the same yesterday, today and forever. Hallowed be Thy name!

I bless Your name, *Jehovah-Jireh,* the One Who sees my needs and provides for them. Hallowed be Thy name!

I bless Your name, *Jehovah-Rapha,* my Healer and the One Who makes bitter experiences sweet. You sent Your Word and healed me. You forgave all my iniquities and You healed all my diseases. Hallowed be Thy name!

I bless Your name, *Jehovah-M'Kaddesh,* the Lord my Sanctifier. You have set me apart for Yourself. Hallowed be Thy name!

Jehovah-Nissi, You are my Victory, my Banner, and my Standard. Your banner over me is love. When the enemy shall come in like a flood, You will lift up a standard against him. Hallowed be Thy name!

Jehovah-Shalom, I bless Your name. You are my Peace — the peace which transcends all understanding, which garrisons and mounts guard over my heart and mind in Christ Jesus. Hallowed be Thy name!

I bless You, *Jehovah-Tsidkenu,* my Righteousness. Thank You for becoming sin for me that I might become the righteousness of God in Christ Jesus. Hallowed be Thy name!

Jehovah-Rohi, You are my Shepherd and I shall not want for any good or beneficial thing. Hallowed be Thy name!

Hallelujah to *Jehovah-Shammah* Who will never leave or forsake me. You are always there. I take comfort and am encouraged and confidently and boldly say, The Lord is my Helper, I will not be seized with alarm — I will not fear or dread or be terrified. What can man do to me? Hallowed be Thy name!

I worship and adore You, *El-Elyon*, the Most High God Who is the First Cause of everything, the Possessor of the heavens and earth. You are the Everlasting-God, the Great-God, the Living-God, the Merciful-God, the Faithful-God, the Mighty-God. You are Truth, Justice, Righteousness, and Perfection. You are *El-Elyon* — the Highest Sovereign of the heavens and the earth. Hallowed be Thy name!

Father, You have exalted above all else Your name and Your Word, and You have magnified Your Word above all Your name! The Word was made flesh, and dwelt among us, and His name is JESUS! Hallowed be Thy name!

Scripture References

Matthew 6:9	Song of Solomon 2:4
Psalm 103:1	Isaiah 59:19
Genesis 1:1,2	Judges 6:24
Psalm 8:5b	Philippians 4:7 AMP
Genesis 49:24,25	Jeremiah 23:5,6
Genesis 15:1,2,8	2 Corinthians 5:21
Hebrews 13:8	Psalm 23:1
Genesis 22:14	Psalm 34:10
Psalm 147:3 AMP	Ezekiel 48:35
Exodus 15:23-26 AMP	Hebrews 13:5
Psalm 107:20	Hebrews 13:6 AMP
Psalm 103:3	Psalm 91:1
Leviticus 20:7,8	Psalm 138:2 AMP
Exodus 17:15	John 1:14

18

DIVINE INTERVENTION
"Thy Kingdom Come"

Father, I pray according to Matthew 6:10, Thy Kingdom come. I am looking for the soon coming of our Lord and Savior Jesus Christ.

Today, we are [even here and] now Your children; it is not yet disclosed (made clear) what we shall be [hereafter], *but we know that when He comes and is manifested we shall [as God's children] resemble and be like Him, for we shall see Him just as He [really] is.* You said that everyone who has this hope [resting] on Him cleanses (purifies) himself just as He is pure — chaste, undefiled, guiltless.

For the grace of God — His unmerited favor and blessing — has come forward (appeared) for the deliverance from sin and the eternal salvation for all mankind. It has trained us to reject and renounce all ungodliness (irreligion) and worldly (passionate) desires, to live discreet (temperate, self-controlled), upright, devout (spiritually whole) lives in this present world, awaiting and looking for the [fulfillment, the realization of our]

73

blessed hope, *even the glorious appearing of our great God and Savior Christ Jesus, the Messiah, the Anointed One.*

For the Lord Himself shall descend from heaven with a shout, with the voice of the archangel, and with the trump of God: and the dead in Christ shall rise first. Then we which are alive and remain shall be caught up together with them in the clouds, to meet the Lord in the air: and so shall we ever be with the Lord.

I thank You, Father, that the Lord shall come (to earth), and all the holy ones [saints and angels] with Him; and the Lord shall be King over all the earth; in that day He shall be one Lord, and His name one. The government shall be upon His shoulder.

Father, I thank You that we shall join the great voices in heaven saying, The kingdoms of this world are become the kingdoms of our Lord, and of His Christ; and He shall reign for ever and ever.

Yours, O Lord, is the greatness, and power, and the glory, and the victory, and the majesty; for all that is in the heavens and the earth is Yours; Yours is the Kingdom, O Lord, and Yours it is to be exalted as head over all. Thy Kingdom come. Hallelujah!

Scripture References

1 John 3:2,3 AMP

Titus 2:11-13 AMP

1 Thessalonians 4:16,17

Zechariah 14:5,9 AMP

Isaiah 9:6 AMP

Revelation 11:15

1 Chronicles 29:11 AMP

19

SUBMISSION
"Thy Will Be Done"

Father, I pray that the will of God be done in my life as it is in heaven. For I am Your [own] handiwork (Your workmanship), recreated in Christ Jesus, [born anew] that I may do those good works which You predestined (planned beforehand) for me, (taking paths which You prepared ahead of time) that I should walk in them — living the good life which You prearranged and made ready for me to live.

Teach me to do Your will, for You are my God; let Your good Spirit lead me into a plain country and into the land of uprightness. Jesus, You gave (yielded) Yourself up [to atone] for my sins (and to save and sanctify me), in order to rescue and deliver me from this present wicked age and world order, in accordance with the will and purpose and plan of our God and Father.

In the name of Jesus, I am not conformed to this world, but am transformed by the renewing of my mind, that I may prove what is that good, and acceptable, and perfect, will of God. For this is the will of God, that I should be consecrated — separated and set apart for pure and holy living: that I should abstain from all sexual vice; that I should know how to possess [control, manage] my own body (in purity, separated from things profane, and) in consecration and honor, not [to be used] in the passion of lust, like the heathen who are ignorant of the true God and have no knowledge of His will.

Father, thank You that You chose me — actually picked me out for Yourself as Your own — in Christ before the foundation of the world; that I should be holy (consecrated and set apart for You) and blameless in Your sight, even above reproach, before You in love: having predestinated me unto the adoption of a child by Jesus Christ to Yourself, according to the good pleasure of Your will.

Your will be done on earth in my life as it is in heaven. Amen and so be it!

Scripture References

Matthew 6:9b,10	Romans 12:2
Ephesians 2:10 AMP	1 Thessalonians 4:4,5 AMP
Psalm 143:10 AMP	Ephesians 1:4 AMP
Galatians 1:4 AMP	Ephesians 1:5

20

PROVISION
"Give Us This Day
Our Daily Bread"

In the name of Jesus, I confess with the Psalmist David, I have not seen the righteous forsaken, nor his seed begging bread.

Father, thank You for food, clothing and shelter. In the name of Jesus, I have stopped being perpetually uneasy (anxious and worried) about my life, what I shall eat and what I shall drink, or about my body, what I shall put on. My life is greater [in quality] than food, and the body [far above and more excellent] than clothing.

The bread of idleness [gossip, discontent and self-pity] I will not eat. It is You, Father, Who will liberally supply (fill to the full) my every need according to Your riches in glory in Christ Jesus.

In the name of Jesus, I shall not live by bread alone, but by every word that proceeds from the mouth of God. Your words were found, and I did eat them, and Your Word was to me a joy and the rejoicing of my heart.

And the Word became flesh, and dwelt among us. Jesus, You are the Bread of Life — that gives me life, the Living Bread.

Thank You, Father, in the name of Jesus, for spiritual bread — manna from heaven.

Scripture References

Matthew 6:9b-11
Psalm 37:25
Matthew 6:25 AMP
Proverbs 31:27b AMP
Philippians 4:19 AMP

Matthew 4:4
Jeremiah 15:16 AMP
John 1:14a
John 6:48-51 AMP

21
Forgiveness
"Forgive Us Our Debts"

Father, I forgive everyone who has trespassed against me so that You can forgive me my trespasses. [Now, having received the Holy Spirit and being led and directed by Him] if I forgive the sins of anyone they are forgiven; if I retain the sins of anyone, they are retained.

Father, Your Word says, **Love your enemies and pray for those who persecute you** (Matt. 5:44 AMP). I come before you in Jesus' name to lift _____ before You. I invoke blessings upon him/her and pray for his/her happiness. I implore Your blessings (favor) upon him/her.

Father, not only will I pray for _____, but I set myself to treat him/her well (do good to, act nobly toward) him/her. I will be merciful, sympathetic, tender, responsive, and compassionate toward _____ even as You are, Father. I am an imitator of You, and I can do all things through Christ Jesus Who strengthens me.

Father, I thank You that I have great peace in this situation, for I love Your law and refuse to take offense toward _____.

Jesus, I am blessed — happy [with life — joy and satisfaction in God's favor and salvation apart from outward conditions] and to be envied — because I take no offense in You and refuse to be hurt or resentful or annoyed or repelled or made to stumble, [whatever may occur].

And now, Father, I roll this work upon You — commit and trust it wholly to You; and believe that You will cause my thoughts to become in agreement to Your will, and so my plans shall be established and succeed.

Scripture References

Matthew 6:12	Ephesians 5:1 AMP
Matthew 6:14,15	Philippians 4:13 AMP
John 20:23 AMP	Psalm 119:165 AMP
Luke 6:27b AMP	Luke 7:23 AMP
Matthew 5:44 AMP	Proverbs 16:3 AMP
Luke 6:28 AMP	

22
GUIDANCE AND
DELIVERANCE
"Lead Us Not Into Temptation"

There has no temptation taken me but such as is common to man: but *God is faithful*, Who will not suffer me to be tempted above that which I am able; but will with the temptation also make a way to escape, that I may be able to bear it.

I count it all joy when I fall into various temptations; knowing this, that the trying of my faith works patience.

I will not say when I am tempted, I am tempted from God; for God is incapable of being tempted by [what is] evil and He Himself tempts no one.

Thank You, Jesus, for giving Yourself for my sins, that You might deliver me from this present evil world, according to the will of God and our Father: to Whom be glory for ever and ever.

Father, in the name of Jesus, and according to the power that is at work in me, I will keep awake (give strict attention, be cautious) and watch and pray that I may not come into temptation. In Jesus' name, amen.

Scripture References

1 Corinthians 10:13	Galatians 1:4,5
James 1:2,3	Ephesians 3:20b
James 1:13 AMP	Matthew 26:41a AMP

23
PRAISE

"For Thine Is the Kingdom, and the Power, and the Glory"

O magnify the Lord with me, and let us exalt His name together.

As for God, His way is perfect! The Word of the Lord is tested and tried; He is a shield to all those who take refuge and put their trust in Him.

Let the words of my mouth and the meditation of my heart be acceptable in Your sight, O Lord, my firm, impenetrable rock and my redeemer.

Your Word has revived me and given me life.

Forever, O Lord, Your Word is settled in heaven.

Your Word is a lamp to my feet and a light to my path.

The sum of Your Word is truth and every one of Your righteous decrees endures forever.

I will worship toward Your holy temple, and praise Your name for Your loving-kindness and for Your truth and faithfulness; for You have exalted above all else Your name and Your Word, and You have magnified Your Word above all Your name!

Let my prayer be set forth as incense before You, the lifting up of my hands as the evening sacrifice. Set a guard, O Lord, before my mouth; keep watch at the door of my lips.

He who brings an offering of praise and thanksgiving honors and glorifies Me; and he who orders his way aright — who prepares the way that I may show him — to him I will demonstrate the salvation of God.

My mouth shall be filled with Your praise and with Your honor all the day.

Because Your loving-kindness is better than life, my lips shall praise You. So will I bless You while I live; I will lift up my hands in Your name.

Your testimonies also are my delight and my counselors.

Scripture References (AMP)

Psalm 34:3	Psalm 138:2
Psalm 18:30	Psalm 141:2,3
Psalm 19:14	Psalm 50:23
Psalm 119:50	Psalm 71:8
Psalm 119:89	Psalm 63,3,4
Psalm 119:105	Psalm 119:24
Psalm 119:160	

24

STRENGTH TO OVERCOME CARES AND BURDENS

Why are you cast down, O my inner self? And why should you moan over me and be disquieted within me?

Father, You set Yourself against the proud and haughty, but give grace [continually] unto the humble. I submit myself therefore to You, God. In the name of Jesus, I resist the devil, and he will flee from me. I resist the devil as he tries to bring worry with the cares of the church to pressure me daily. Except the Lord builds the house, they labor in vain who build it.

Jesus, I come to You, for I labor and am heavy-laden and over burdened, and You cause me to rest — You will ease and relieve and refresh my soul. I take Your Yoke upon me, and I learn of You; for You are gentle (meek) and humble (lowly) in heart, and I will find rest — relief, ease and refreshment and recreation and blessed quiet — for my soul. For Your yoke is wholesome (*easy*) — not harsh, hard, sharp or pressing, but comfortable, gracious and pleasant; and Your burden is light and easy to be borne.

86

I cast my burden on You, Lord, [releasing the weight of it] and You will sustain me; I thank You that You will never allow me, the [consistently] righteous, to be moved — made to slip, fall or fail.

In the name of Jesus, I withstand the devil. I am firm in my faith [against his onset] — rooted, established, strong, immovable and determined. I cease from [the weariness and pain] of human labor; and am zealous and exert myself and strive diligently to enter into the rest [of God] — to know and experience it for myself.

Father, I thank You that Your presence goes with me, and that You give me rest. I am still and rest in You, Lord; I wait for You, and patiently stay myself upon You. I will not fret myself, nor shall I let my heart be troubled, neither shall I let it be afraid. I hope in You, God, and wait expectantly for You; for I shall yet praise You, for You are the help of my countenance, and my God.

Scripture References (AMP)

Psalm 42:11a	Hebrews 4:10b,11
James 4:6,7	Exodus 33:14
Psalm 127:1a	Psalm 37:7
Matthew 11:28-30	John 14:27b
Psalm 55:22	Psalm 42:11b
1 Peter 5:9a	

25
CONQUERING THE THOUGHT LIFE

In the name of Jesus, I take authority over my thought life. Even though I walk (live) in the flesh, I am not carrying on my warfare according to the flesh and using mere human weapons. For the weapons of my warfare are not physical (weapons of flesh and blood), but they are mighty before God for the overthrow and destruction of strongholds. I refute arguments and theories and reasonings and every proud and lofty thing that sets itself up against the (true) knowledge of God; and I lead every thought and purpose away captive into the obedience of Christ, the Messiah, the Anointed One.

With my soul I will bless the Lord with every thought and purpose in life. My mind will not wander out of the presence of God. My life shall glorify the Father — *spirit, soul, and body.* I take no account of the evil done to me — I pay no attention to a suffered wrong. It holds no place in my thought life. I am ever ready to believe the best of every person. I gird up the loins of my mind, and I set my mind and keep it set on what is above — the higher things — not on the things that are on the earth.

Whatever is true, whatever is worthy of reverence and is honorable and seemly, whatever is just, whatever is pure, whatever is lovely and lovable, whatever is kind and winsome and gracious, if there is any virtue and excellence, if there is anything worthy of praise, I will think on and weigh and take account of these things — I will fix my mind on them.

The carnal mind is no longer operative for I have the mind of Christ, the Messiah, and do hold the thoughts (feelings and purposes) of His heart. In the name of Jesus, I will practice what I have learned and received and heard and seen in Christ, and model my way of living on it, and the God of peace — of untroubled, undisturbed well-being — will be with me.

Scripture References (AMP)

2 Corinthians 10:3-5
Psalm 103:1
1 Corinthians 6:20
1 Corinthians 13:5b,7a
1 Peter 1:13

Colossians 3:2
Philippians 4:8
1 Corinthians 2:16
Philippians 4:9

26
Godly Wisdom in the Affairs of Life

Father, You said if anyone lacks wisdom, let him ask of You, Who giveth to all men liberally, and upbraideth not; and it shall be given him. Therefore, I ask in faith, nothing wavering, to be filled with the knowledge of Your will in all wisdom and spiritual understanding. Today I incline my ear unto wisdom, and apply my heart to understanding so that I might receive that which has been freely given unto me.

In the name of Jesus, I receive skill and godly wisdom and instruction. I discern and comprehend the words of understanding and insight. I receive instruction in wise dealing and the discipline of wise thoughtfulness, righteousness, justice, and integrity.

Prudence, knowledge, discretion, and discernment are given to me. I increase in knowledge. As a person of understanding, I acquire skill and attain to sound counsels [so that I may be able to steer my course rightly].

Wisdom will keep, defend, and protect me; I love her and she guards me. I prize Wisdom highly and exalt her; she will bring me to honor because I embrace her. She gives to my head a wreath of gracefulness; a crown of beauty and glory will she deliver to me. Length of days is in her right hand, and in her left hand are riches and honor.

Jesus has been made unto me wisdom, and in Him are all the treasures of [divine] wisdom, [of comprehensive insight into the ways and purposes of God], and [all the riches of spiritual] knowledge and enlightenment are stored up and lie hidden. God has hidden away sound and godly wisdom and stored it up for me, for I am the righteousness of God in Christ Jesus.

Therefore, I will walk in paths of uprightness. When I walk, my steps shall not be hampered — my path will be clear and open; and when I run I shall not stumble. I take fast hold of instruction, and do not let her go; I guard her, for she is my life. I let my eyes look right on [with fixed purpose], and my gaze is straight before me. I consider well the path of my feet, and I let all my ways be established and ordered aright.

Father, in the name of Jesus, I look carefully to how I walk! I live purposefully and worthily and accurately, not as unwise and witless, but as

a wise — sensible, intelligent person; making the
very most of my time — buying up every
opportunity.

Scripture References

James 1:5,6a

Colossians 1:9b

Proverbs 2:2

Proverbs 1:2-5 AMP

Proverbs 4:6,8,9 AMP

Proverbs 3:16 AMP

1 Corinthians 1:30

Colossians 2:3 AMP

Proverbs 2:7 AMP

2 Corinthians 5:21

Proverbs 4:11-13,25,26 AMP

Ephesians 5:15,16 AMP

27
THE SETTING OF
PROPER PRIORITIES

Father, in the name of Jesus, I come before You. Spirit of Truth, Who comes from the Father, it is You Who guides me into all truth. According to 3 John 2 it is God's will that I prosper in every way and that my body keeps well, even as my soul keeps well and prospers.

One thing I ask of You, Lord, one thing will I seek after, inquire for and [insistently] require, that I may dwell in Your house [in Your presence], all the days of my life, to behold and gaze upon Your beauty. I come to meditate, consider and inquire in Your temple *(about success in life)*.

Father, You have said, **I will not in any way fail you nor give you up nor leave you without support. [I will] not, [I will] not, [I will] not in any degree leave you helpless, nor forsake nor let [you] down, [relax my hold on you]. — Assuredly not** (Heb. 13:5 AMP)! So I take comfort and am encouraged and confidently and boldly say that the Lord is my Helper, I will not be seized

93

with alarm — I will not fear or dread or be terrified. What can man do to me?

In the name of Jesus, I am strong and very courageous, that I may do according to all Your Word. I turn not from it to the right hand or to the left, that I may prosper wherever I go. The Word of God shall not depart out of my mouth, but I shall meditate on it day and night. I hear therefore and am watchful to keep the instructions, the laws and precepts of my Lord God, that it may be well with me and that I may increase exceedingly, as the Lord God has promised me, in a land flowing with milk and honey. The Lord my God is one Lord — the only Lord. And I shall love the Lord my God with all my [mind and] heart, and with my entire being, and with all my might. And I will love my neighbor as myself.

Jesus, You said that when I do this I will live — enjoy active, blessed, endless life in the Kingdom of God. Therefore, I will not worry or be anxious about what I am going to eat, or what I am going to have to drink, or what I am going to have to wear. My heavenly Father knows that I need them all. But I purpose in my heart to seek for (aim at and strive after) first of all Your Kingdom, Lord, and Your righteousness [Your way of doing and being right], and then all these things taken together will be given me besides.

Now thanks be to You, Father, Who always causes me to triumph in Christ!

Scripture References

John 16:13a	Deuteronomy 6:1,3-5 AMP
Psalm 27:4 AMP	Luke 10:27,28 AMP
Hebrews 13:5b,6 AMP	Matthew 6:31-33 AMP
Joshua 1:7,8a AMP	2 Corinthians 2:14

28
KNOWING GOD'S WILL

Father, I thank You that You are instructing me in the way which I should go and that You are guiding me with Your eye. I thank You for Your guidance and leading concerning Your will, Your plan, and Your purpose for my life. I do hear the voice of the Good Shepherd, for I know You and follow You. You lead me in the paths of righteousness for Your name's sake.

Thank You, Father, that my path is growing brighter and brighter until it reaches the full light of day. As I follow You, Lord, I believe my path is becoming clearer each day.

Thank You, Father, that Jesus was made unto me wisdom. Confusion is not a part of my life. I am not confused about Your will for my life. I trust in You and lean not unto my own understanding. As I acknowledge You in all my ways, You are directing my paths. I believe that as I trust in You completely, You will show me the path of life.

Scripture References

Psalm 32:8　　　　1 Corinthians 1:30
John 10:3,4　　　　1 Corinthians 14:33
Psalm 23:3　　　　Proverbs 3:5,6
Proverbs 4:18　　　Psalm 16:11
Ephesians 5:19

29

THE NEW CREATION MARRIAGE

Introduction

The harmony and unity in a church will never exceed the harmony and unity in the homes represented in the congregation. Each household actually should be a mini-church coming together to form a body of believers. Love must originate from God the Father. For years I gave glory to the Lord for the love and peace of God which reigned supreme in our home. Many times circumstances said, "It isn't so"; God, however, watched over His Word to perform it in our lives.

You become a doer of the Word in your own home by obeying the Royal Law of Love. God is looking within each family for one intercessor who will "stand in the gap" and "put up a hedge" for the entire household. I encourage you to be that one who makes the decision to be subject to God for the purpose of peace, harmony, and unity. Stand firm against the devil: resist him, and he will flee from your family.

The following prayer was given to me by the Holy Spirit for my husband and me.

Husband, you may pray the part for the wife in the third person.

Wife, you may pray the part for the husband in the third person.

Find time to pray together, if both parties are willing and receptive.

Prayer

The couple prays together:

Father, in the name of Jesus, we rejoice and delight ourselves in one another. We are in Christ, the Messiah, and have become (new creatures altogether), new creations; the old (previous moral and spiritual condition) has passed away. Behold, the fresh and new has come! May our family be seen as bright lights — stars or beacons shining out clearly — in the [dark] world.

The husband prays:

I love my wife, as Christ loves the Church. I am to her what Christ is to the Church. I have given myself up for her, so that I might set her apart for myself, having cleansed her by the washing of water with the Word through intercession and counsel, that I might present her to myself in glorious splendor, for she is [the expression of] my glory (majesty, pre-eminence). Therefore, she is without spot or wrinkle or any such things — but she is holy and faultless as my help meet. I love her as [being in a sense] my own body, for I love her as I love myself. I nourish and carefully protect and cherish her, as Christ does the Church, for we are members (parts) of His body. Jesus is my example. I trust [myself and everything] to God Who judges fairly.

I thank You, Father, that my wife and I are able ministers of the New Covenant — ministers of reconciliation. Father, [in Your love] You chose us — actually picked us out for Yourself as Your own — in Christ before the foundation of the world; that we should be holy (consecrated and set apart for Yourself) before You in love.

Father, my wife and I have received Your favor and mercy which You have lavished upon us in every kind of wisdom and understanding (practical insight and prudence).

The wife prays:

Father, in the name of Jesus, I am submissive — I submit and adapt myself — to my own husband as [a service] to the Lord. I see that I respect and reverence my husband — that I notice him, regard him, honor him, prefer him, venerate and esteem him; and that I defer to him, praise him, and love and admire him exceedingly. The heart of my husband can trust in me confidently and rely on and believe in me safely, so that he has no lack of honest gain or need of dishonest spoil. I will comfort, encourage and do him only good as long as there is life within me.

As I seek counsel from my husband, he will be my strength, my hiding place, my high tower, my intercessor — and we will stand side by side as we minister life, love, healing — soundness and wholeness — to those God sends our way. We will stand together as one before the Body of Christ.

Scripture References

2 Corinthians 5:17 AMP
Philippians 2:15b AMP
Ephesians 5:25-30 AMP
1 Peter 2:23b AMP
2 Corinthians 3:6
2 Corinthians 5:18

Ephesians 1:4,6,8 AMP
Ephesians 5:22,33b AMP
1 Corinthians 11:7b AMP
Proverbs 31:11,12 AMP
Matthew 19:5,6 AMP

30
HARMONIOUS MARRIAGE

Father, in the name of Jesus, it is written in Your Word that love is shed abroad in our hearts by the Holy Ghost Who is given to us. Because You are in us, we acknowledge that love reigns supreme. We believe that love is displayed in full expression enfolding and knitting us together in truth, making us perfect for every good work to do Your will, working in us that which is pleasing in Your sight.

We live and conduct ourselves and our marriage honorably and becomingly. We esteem it as precious, worthy, and of great price. *We commit ourselves to live in mutual harmony and accord with one another* delighting in each other, being of the same mind and united in spirit.

Father, we believe and say that we are gentle, compassionate, courteous, tender-hearted, and humble-minded. We seek peace, and it keeps our hearts in quietness and assurance. Because we follow after love and dwell in peace, our prayers are not hindered in any way, in the name of Jesus. We are heirs together of the grace of God.

Our marriage grows stronger day by day in the bond of unity because it is founded on Your Word and rooted and grounded in Your love. Father, we thank You for the performance of it, in Jesus' name.

Scripture References

Romans 5:5	Ephesians 4:32
Philippians 1:9	Isaiah 32:17
Colossians 3:14	Philippians 4:7
Colossians 1:10	1 Peter 3:7
Philippians 2:13	Ephesians 3:17,18
Philippians 2:2	Jeremiah 1:12

31

COMPATIBILITY IN MARRIAGE

Father, in the name of Jesus, I pray and confess that my spouse and I endure long and are patient and kind; that we are never envious and never boil over with jealousy. We are not boastful or vainglorious, and we do not display ourselves haughtily. We are not conceited or arrogant and inflated with pride.

We are not rude and unmannerly, and we do not act unbecomingly. We do not insist on our own rights or our own way, for we are not self-seeking or touchy or fretful or resentful.

We take no account of the evil done to us and pay no attention to a suffered wrong. We do not rejoice at injustice and unrighteousness, but we rejoice when right and truth prevail.

We bear up under anything and everything that comes. We are ever ready to believe the best of each other. Our hopes are fadeless under all circumstances. We endure everything without weakening. *Our love never fails* — it never fades out or becomes obsolete or comes to an end.

We are confessing that our lives and our family's lives lovingly express truth in all things that we speak truly, deal truly, and live truly. We are enfolded in love and have grown up in every way and in all things. We esteem and delight in one another, forgiving one another readily and freely as God in Christ has forgiven us. We are imitators of God and copy His example as well-beloved children imitate their father.

Thank You, Father, that our marriage grows stronger each day because it is founded on Your Word and on Your kind of love. We give You the praise for it all, Father, in the name of Jesus.

Scripture References

1 Corinthians 13:4-8 AMP	Ephesians 4:15,32
1 Corinthians 14:1	Ephesians 5:1,2

32

THE CHILDREN

Father, in the name of Jesus, I pray and confess Your Word over my children and surround them with my faith — faith in Your Word that You watch over it to perform it! I confess and believe that my children are disciples of Christ taught of the Lord and obedient to Your will. Great is the peace and undisturbed composure of my children, because You, God, contend with that which contends with my children, and You give them safety and ease them.

Father, You will perfect that which concerns me. *I commit and cast the care of my children once and for all over on You, Father.* They are in Your hands, and I am positively persuaded that You are able to guard and keep that which I have committed to You. You are more than enough!

I confess that my children obey their parents in the Lord as His representatives, because this is just and right. My children _____ honor, esteem, and value as precious their parents; for this is the first commandment with a promise: that all may be well with my children

106

and that they may live long on earth. I believe and confess that my children choose life and love You, Lord, obey Your voice, and cling to You; for You are their life and the length of their days. Therefore, my children are the head and not the tail, and shall be above only and not beneath. They are blessed when they come in and when they go out.

I believe and confess that You give Your angels charge over my children to accompany and defend and preserve them in all their ways. You, Lord, are their refuge and fortress. You are their glory and the lifter of their heads.

As parents, we will not provoke, irritate, or fret our children. We will not be hard on them or harass them, or cause them to become discouraged, sullen, or morose, or feel inferior and frustrated. We will not break or wound their spirits, but we will rear them tenderly in the training, discipline, counsel, and admonition of the Lord. We will train them in the way they should go, and when they are old they will not depart from it.

O Lord, my Lord, how excellent (majestic and glorious) is Your name in all the earth! You have set Your glory on or above the heavens. Out of the mouth of babes and unweaned infants You have established strength because of Your foes, that You might silence the enemy and the avenger. I sing praise to Your name, O Most High. *The enemy is turned back from my children in the name of Jesus!* They increase in wisdom and in favor with God and man.

Scripture References

Jeremiah 1:12	Psalm 91:11
Isaiah 54:13	Psalm 91:2
Isaiah 49:25	Psalm 3:3
1 Peter 5:7	Colossians 3:21
2 Timothy 1:12	Ephesians 6:4
Ephesians 6:1-3	Proverbs 22:6
Deuteronomy 30:19,20	Psalm 8:1,2
Deuteronomy 28:13	Psalm 9:2,3
Deuteronomy 28:3,6	Luke 2:52

33
T HE HOME

Father, I thank You that You have blessed me with all spiritual blessings in Christ Jesus.

Through skillful and godly wisdom is my house (my life, my home, my family) built, and by understanding it is established on a sound and good foundation. And by knowledge shall the chambers (of its every area) be filled with all precious and pleasant riches — great priceless treasure. The house of the uncompromisingly righteous shall stand. Prosperity and welfare are in my house in the name of Jesus.

My house is securely built. It is founded on a rock — revelation knowledge of Your Word, Father. Jesus is my Cornerstone. Jesus is Lord of my household. Jesus is our Lord — spirit, soul, and body.

Whatever may be our task, we work at it heartily as something done for You, Lord, and not for men. We love each other with the God kind of love, and we dwell in peace. My home is deposited into Your charge, entrusted to Your protection and care.

Father, as for me and my house we shall serve the Lord in Jesus' name. Hallelujah!

Scripture References

Ephesians 1:3

Proverbs 24:3,4 AMP

Proverbs 15:6

Proverbs 12:7 AMP

Psalm 112:3

Luke 6:48

Acts 4:11

Acts 16:31

Philippians 2:10,11

Colossians 3:23

Colossians 3:14,15

Acts 20:32

Joshua 24:15

34
Prosperity

Father, in the name of Your Son, Jesus, I confess Your Word over my finances this day. As I do this, I say it with my mouth and believe it in my heart and know that Your Word will not return to You void, but will accomplish what it says it will do.

Therefore, I believe in the name of Jesus that all my needs are met, according to Philippians 4:19. I believe that because I have given tithes and offerings to further your cause, Father, gifts will be given to me, good measure, pressed down, shaken together, and running over will they pour into my bosom. For with the measure I deal out, it will be measured back to me.

Father, You have delivered me out of the authority of darkness into the Kingdom of Your dear Son. Father, I have taken my place as your child. I thank You that You have assumed Your place as my Father and have made Your home with me. You are taking care of me and even now are enabling me to walk in love and in wisdom, and to walk in the fullness of fellowship with Your Son.

Satan, I bind you from my finances, according to Matthew 18:18, and loose you from your assignment against me, in the name of Jesus.

Father, I thank You that Your ministering spirits are now free to minister for me and bring in the necessary finances.

Father, I confess You are a very present help in trouble, and You are more than enough. I confess, God, You are able to make all grace — every favor and earthly blessing — come to me in abundance, so that I am always, and in all circumstances furnished in abundance for every good work and charitable donation.

Scripture References

Isaiah 55:11
Philippians 4:19
Luke 6:38
Mark 10:29,30
Colossians 1:13

2 Corinthians 6:16,18
Matthew 18:18
Hebrews 1:14
2 Corinthians 9:8 AMP
Psalm 46:1

35

Dedication for your Tithes

I profess this day unto the Lord God that I have come into the inheritance which the Lord swore to give me. I am in the land which You have provided for me in Jesus Christ, the Kingdom of Almighty God. I was a sinner serving Satan; he was my god. But I called upon the name of Jesus, and You heard my cry and delivered me into the Kingdom of Your dear Son.

Jesus, as my Lord and High Priest, I bring the first fruits of my income to You and worship the Lord my God with it.

I rejoice in all the good which You have given to me and my household. I have hearkened to the voice of the Lord my God and have done according to all that He has commanded me. Now look down from your holy habitation from heaven and bless me as You said in Your Word. I thank You, Father, in Jesus' name.

Scripture References

Deuteronomy 26:1,3,10,11,14,15 AMP   Colossians 1:13
Ephesians 2:1-5

36
Health and Healing

Father, in the name of Jesus, I confess Your Word concerning healing. As I do this, I believe and say that Your Word will not return to You void, but will accomplish what it says it will. Therefore, I believe in the name of Jesus that I am healed, according to 1 Peter 2:24. It is written in Your Word that Jesus himself took our infirmities and bore our sicknesses. Therefore, with great boldness and confidence I say on the authority of that written Word that I am redeemed from the curse of sickness, and I refuse to tolerate its symptoms.

Satan, I speak to you in the name of Jesus and say that your principalities, powers, your spirits who rule the present darkness, and your spiritual wickedness in heavenly places are bound from operating against me in any way. I am the property of Almighty God, and I give you no place in me. I dwell in the secret place of the Most High God. I abide, remain stable and fixed under the shadow of the Almighty, whose power no foe can withstand.

114

Now, Father, because I reverence and worship You, I have the assurance of Your Word that the angel of the Lord encamps around about me and delivers me from every evil work. No evil shall befall me, no plague or calamity shall come near my dwelling. I confess the Word of God abides in me and delivers to me perfect soundness of mind and wholeness in body and spirit from the deepest parts of my nature in my immortal spirit even to the joints and marrow of my bones. That Word is medication and life to my flesh for the law of the Spirit of life operates in me and makes me free from the law of sin and death.

I have on the whole armor of God, and the shield of faith protects me from all the fiery darts of the wicked. Jesus is the High Priest of my confession, and I hold fast to my confession of faith in Your Word. I stand immovable and fixed in full assurance that I have health and healing now in the name of Jesus.

Once this has been prayed, thank the Father that Satan is bound and continue to confess this healing and thank God for it.

Scripture References

Isaiah 55:11	Psalm 91:10
1 Peter 2:24	Psalm 34:7
Matthew 8:17	2 Timothy 1:7
Galatians 3:13	Hebrews 4:12,14
James 4:7	Proverbs 4:22
Ephesians 6:12	Romans 8:2
2 Corinthians 10:4	Ephesians 6:11,16
Psalm 91:1	Psalm 112:7

S³⁷AFETY

Father, in the name of Jesus, I thank You that You watch over Your Word to perform it. I thank You that I dwell in the secret place of the Most High and that I remain stable and fixed under the shadow of the Almighty whose power no foe can withstand.

Father, You are my refuge and my fortress. *No evil shall befall me — no accident shall overtake me — nor any plague or calamity come near my home.* You give Your angels special charge over me, to accompany and defend and preserve me in all my ways of obedience and service. They are encamped around about me.

Father, You are my confidence, firm and strong. You keep my foot from being caught in a trap or hidden danger. Father, You give me safety and ease me — *Jesus is my safety!*

Traveling — As I go, I say, "Let me pass over to the other side," and I have what I say. I walk on my way securely and in confident trust, for my heart and mind are firmly fixed and stayed on You, and I am kept in perfect peace.

Sleeping — Father, I sing for joy upon my bed because You sustain me. In peace I lie down and sleep, for You alone, Lord, make me dwell in safety. I lie down and I am not afraid. My sleep is sweet for You give blessings to me in sleep. Thank You, Father, in Jesus' name. Amen.

Continue to feast and meditate upon all of Psalm 91 for yourself and your loved ones!

Scripture References

Jeremiah 1:12	Proverbs 3:23 AMP
Psalm 91:1,2 AMP	Psalm 112:7
Psalm 91:10 AMP	Isaiah 26:3
Psalm 91:11 AMP	Psalm 149:5
Psalm 34:7	Psalm 3:5
Proverbs 3:26 AMP	Psalm 4:8 AMP
Isaiah 49:25	Proverbs 3:24
Mark 4:35 AMP	Psalm 127:2

38
Peaceful Sleep

In the name of Jesus, I bind you, Satan, and all your agents from my dreams. I forbid you to interfere in any way with my sleep.

I bring every thought, every imagination, and every dream into the captivity and obedience of Jesus Christ. Father, I thank You that even as I sleep my heart counsels me and reveals to me Your purpose and plan. Thank You for sweet sleep, for You promised Your beloved sweet sleep. Therefore, my heart is glad, and my spirit rejoices. My body and soul rest and confidently dwell in safety.

Scripture References

Matthew 16:19   Psalm 16:7-9
Matthew 18:18   Psalm 127:2
2 Corinthians 10:5   Proverbs 3:24

39

VICTORY OVER PRIDE

Father, Your Word says that You hate a proud look, that You resist the proud but give grace to the humble. I submit myself therefore to You, God. In the name of Jesus, I resist the devil, and he will flee from me. I renounce every manifestation of pride in my life as sin; I repent and turn from it.

As an act of faith, I clothe myself with humility and receive Your grace. I humble myself under Your mighty hand, Lord, that You may exalt me in due time. I refuse to exalt myself. I do not think of myself more highly than I ought; I do not have an exaggerated opinion of my own importance, but rate my ability with sober judgment, according to the degree of faith apportioned to me.

Proverbs 11:2 says, When pride cometh, then cometh shame: but with the lowly is wisdom. Father, I set myself to resist pride when it comes. My desire is to be counted among the lowly, so I take on the attitude of a servant.

Father, thank You that You dwell with him who is of a contrite and humble spirit. You revive the spirit of the humble and revive the heart of the contrite ones. Thank You that the reward of humility and the reverent and worshipful fear of the Lord is riches and honor and life.

Scripture References

Proverbs 6:16	Proverbs 11:2
James 4:6,7	Matthew 23:11
Proverbs 21:4	Isaiah 57:15
1 Peter 5:5,6	Proverbs 22:4 AMP
Romans 12:3 AMP	

40
VICTORY OVER FEAR

Father, in Jesus' name, I confess and believe that no weapon formed against me shall prosper, and any tongue that rises against me in judgment I shall show to be in the wrong. I believe I dwell in the secret place of the Most High. I shall remain stable and fixed under the shadow of the Almighty God whose power no foe can withstand — this secret place hides me from the strife of tongues.

I believe the wisdom of God's Word dwells in me, and because it does, I realize that I am without fear or dread of evil. In all my ways I know and acknowledge God and His Word; thus, He directs and makes straight and plain my pathway. As I attend to God's Word, it is health to my nerves and sinews, and marrow and moistening to my bones.

I am strengthened and reinforced with mighty power in my innerself by the Holy Spirit Himself Who dwells in me. God is my strength and my refuge, and I confidently trust in Him and in His Word. I am empowered through my union with

Almighty God. This gives me the superhuman, supernatural strength to walk in divine health and to live in abundance.

God Himself has said, **I will never leave you without support or forsake you or let you down, my child. [I will] not, [I will] not, [I will] not in any degree leave you helpless or relax my hold on you...assuredly not!** (Heb. 13:5 AMP)

I take comfort and am encouraged and confidently and boldly say, "The Lord is my helper. I will not be seized with alarm. I will not fear or be terrified, for what can man do to me?"

I confess and believe that my children are disciples taught of the Lord and obedient to God's will. Great is the peace and undisturbed composure of my children — because God Himself contends with that which contends with me and my children, and He gives them safety and eases them. God will perfect that which concerns me.

This Word of God that I have spoken is alive and full of power. It is active and operative. It energizes me, and it affects me. As I speak God's Word, it is sharper than any two-edged sword, and it is penetrating into my joints and into the marrow of my bones. It is healing to my flesh. It is prosperity for me. It is the magnificent Word of Almighty God. According to His Word that I have spoken, so be it! Hallelujah!

Scripture References

Isaiah 54:17 AMP
Psalm 91:1 AMP
Psalm 31:20
Proverbs 3:6,8 AMP
Ephesians 3:16 AMP
Psalm 91:2

Ephesians 6:10 AMP
Hebrews 13:5,6 AMP
Isaiah 54:13 AMP
Isaiah 49:25 AMP
Psalm 138:8 AMP
Hebrews 4:12 AMP

41
Victory over Depression

Father, You are my refuge and my high tower and my stronghold in times of trouble. I lean on and confidently put my trust in You, for You have not forsaken me. I seek You on the authority of Your Word and the right of my necessity. I praise You, the help of my countenance and my God.

Lord, You lift up those who are bowed down. Therefore, I am strong and my heart takes courage. I establish myself on righteousness — right standing in conformity with Your will and order. I am far even from the thought of oppression or destruction, for I fear not. I am far from terror, for it shall not come near me.

Father, You have thoughts and plans for my welfare and peace. *My mind is stayed on You,* for I stop allowing myself to be agitated and disturbed and intimidated and cowardly and unsettled.

Satan, I resist you and every oppressive spirit in the näme of Jesus. I resist fear, discouragement, self-pity, and depression. I speak the Word of truth, in the power of God, and I give you no place, Satan; I give no opportunity to you. I am delivered from oppression by the Blood of the Lamb.

Father, I thank You that I have been given a spirit of power and of love and of a calm and well-balanced mind. I have discipline and self-control. I have the mind of Christ and hold the thoughts, feelings, and purposes of His heart. I have a fresh mental and spiritual attitude, for I am constantly renewed in the spirit of my mind with Your Word, Father.

Therefore, I brace up and reinvigorate and cut through and make firm and straight paths for my feet — safe and upright and happy paths that go in the right direction. I arise from the depression and prostration in which circumstances have kept me. I rise to new life, I shine and am radiant with the glory of the Lord.

Thank You, Father, in Jesus' name that I am set free from every evil work. I praise You that the joy of the Lord is my strength and stronghold! Hallelujah!

Scripture References

Psalm 9:9,10 AMP

Psalm 146:8

Psalm 31:24 AMP

Isaiah 35:3,4

Isaiah 54:14

Isaiah 50:10

Jeremiah 29:11-13 AMP

Isaiah 26:3

John 14:27 AMP

James 4:7

Ephesians 4:27

Luke 4:18,19

2 Timothy 1:7 AMP

1 Corinthians 2:16 AMP

Philippians 2:5

Ephesians 4:23,24 AMP

Hebrews 12:12,13 AMP

Isaiah 60:1 AMP

Galatians 1:4

Nehemiah 8:10 AMP

42

UNITY AND HARMONY

Father, in the name of Jesus, this is the confidence that we have in You, that, if we ask anything according to Your will, You hear us: and since we know that You hear us, whatsoever we ask, we know that we have the petitions that we desire of You.

Father, You said, **Behold, they are of one people, and they have all one language; and this is only the beginning of what they will do; and now nothing they have imagined they can do will be impossible to them** (Gen. 11:6 AMP). We pray by the name of our Lord Jesus, that all of us in Your Body be in perfect harmony, and full agreement in what we say, and that there be no dissensions or factions or divisions among us; but that we be perfectly united in our common understanding and in our opinions and judgments.

Holy Spirit, teach us how to agree (harmonize together, together make a symphony) about — anything and everything — so that whatever we ask will come to pass and be done for us by our Father in heaven.

We pray that as members of the Body of Christ we will live as becomes us — with complete lowliness of mind (humility) and meekness (unselfishness, gentleness, mildness), with patience, bearing with one another and making allowances because we love one another. In the name of Jesus, we are eager and strive earnestly to guard and keep the harmony and oneness of [produced by] the Spirit in the binding power of peace.

We commit, in the name of Jesus, and according to the power of God at work in us, to be of one and the same mind (united in spirit), sympathizing [with one another], loving [each the others] as brethren (of one household), compassionate and courteous — tenderhearted and humble-minded. We will never return evil for evil or insult for insult — scolding, tongue-lashing, berating; but on the contrary blessing — praying for their welfare, happiness, and protection, and truly pitying and loving one another. For we know that to this we have been called, that we may ourselves inherit a blessing [from God] — obtain a blessing as heirs, bringing welfare and happiness and protection.

Father, thank You that Jesus has given to us the glory and honor which You gave Him, that we may be one, [even] as You and Jesus are one: Jesus in us and You in Jesus, in order that we may become one and perfectly united, that the world may know and [definitely] recognize that You sent

Jesus, and that You have loved them [even] as You have loved Jesus.

Father, Thy will be done in earth, as it is in heaven. Amen, and so be it.

Scripture References

1 John 5:14,15
Genesis 11:6 AMP
1 Corinthians 1:10 AMP
Matthew 18:19 AMP

Ephesians 4:2,3 AMP
1 Peter 3:8,9 AMP
John 17:22,23 AMP
Matthew 6:10b

43

SCHOOL SYSTEMS AND CHILDREN

Father, we thank You that the entrance of Your Word brings light and thank You that You watch over Your Word to perform it. Father, we bring before You the _____ school system(s) and the men and women who are in positions of authority within the school system(s).

We believe that skillful and godly wisdom has entered into their hearts; that Your knowledge is pleasant to them. Discretion watches over them; understanding keeps them and delivers them from the way of evil and from evil men. We pray that men and women of integrity, blameless, and complete in Your sight, remain in these positions, but that the wicked be cut off and the treacherous be rooted out in the name of Jesus. Father, we thank You for born-again, Spirit-filled people in these positions.

Father, we bring our children, our young people before You. We speak forth Your Word boldly and confidently, Father, that we and our households are saved in the name of Jesus. We are redeemed from the curse of the law for Jesus was made a curse for us. *Our sons and daughters are not given to another people*. We enjoy our children, and they shall not go into captivity, in the name of Jesus.

As parents, we train our children in the way they should go, and when they are old they shall not depart from it.

Our children shrink from whatever might offend You, Father, and discredit the name of Christ. They show themselves to be blameless, guileless, innocent, and uncontaminated children of God without blemish (faultless, unrebukable) in the midst of a crooked and wicked generation, holding out to it and offering to all the Word of Life. Thank You, Father, that You give them knowledge and skill in all learning and wisdom, and bring them into favor with those around them.

Father, we pray and intercede that these young people, their parents, and the leaders in the school system(s) separate themselves from contact with contaminating and corrupting influences. They cleanse themselves from everything that would contaminate and defile their spirits, souls, and bodies. We confess that they shun immorality and all sexual looseness — flee from impurity in thought, word or deed. They live and conduct themselves honorably and becomingly as in the open light of day. We confess and believe that they

132

shun youthful lusts and flee from them in the name of Jesus.

Satan, we speak to you in the name of Jesus. We bind you, the principalities, the powers, the rulers of the darkness, and wicked spirits in heavenly places and tear down strongholds using the mighty weapons God has provided for us in the name of Jesus. We bind up that blinding spirit of antichrist. We bind every spirit of the occult — astrology, witchcraft, every familiar spirit. We bind sexual immorality, idolatry, obscenity, and profanity. We bind those spirits of alcohol, nicotine, and drug addiction. We bind worldly wisdom in any form — every opposer to the truth. We bind every destructive, deceitful, thieving spirit. You are loosed from your assignment against _____ in the name of Jesus for they escape from the snare of the devil who has held them captive.

We commission the ministering spirits to go forth and police the area dispelling the forces of darkness.

Father, we thank You that in Christ all the treasures of divine wisdom (of comprehensive insight into the ways and purposes of God) and all the riches of spiritual knowledge and enlightenment are stored up and lie hidden for us, and we walk in Him.

We praise You, Father, that we shall see _____ walking in the ways of piety and virtue, revering Your name, Father. Those who err in spirit will come to understanding and those who murmur discontentedly will accept instruction in the Way, Jesus, to Your will and carry out Your purposes in their lives, for You, Father, occupy first place in their hearts. We surround _____ with our faith.

Thank you, Father, that You are the delivering God. Thank You, that the good news of the Gospel is published throughout our school system(s). Thank You, for intercessors to stand on Your Word and for laborers of the harvest to preach Your Word in Jesus' name. Praise the Lord!

Scripture References

Psalm 119:130
Jeremiah 1:12
Proverbs 2:10-12 AMP
Proverbs 2:21,22 AMP
Acts 16:31
Galatians 3:13
Deuteronomy 28:32,41
Proverbs 22:6 AMP
Philippians 2:15,16 AMP
Daniel 1:17 AMP
Daniel 1:9
1 John 2:17 AMP

2 Timothy 2:21 AMP
2 Corinthians 7:1 AMP
1 Corinthians 6:18 AMP
Romans 13:13 AMP
Ephesians 5:4
2 Timothy 2:22
Matthew 18:18
2 Timothy 2:26
Hebrews 1:14
Colossians 2:3 AMP
Isaiah 29:23,24 AMP

44
Salvation

Father, in the name of Jesus, we come before You in prayer and in faith, believing. It is written in Your Word that Jesus came to save the lost. You wish all men to be saved and to know Your Divine Truth, Therefore, Father, we bring _____ before You this day.

Satan, we bind you in the name of Jesus and loose you from the activities in _____ *'s life!*

Father, we ask the Lord of the harvest to thrust the perfect laborer into his/her path, a laborer to share Your Gospel in a special way so that he/she will listen and understand it. As Your laborer ministers to him/her, we believe that he/she will come to his/her senses...come out of the snare of the devil who has held him/her captive and make Jesus the Lord of his/her life.

Your Word says that You will deliver those for whom we intercede, who are not innocent, through the cleanness *of our hands.* We're standing on Your Word, and from this moment on, Father, we shall praise You and thank You for his/her salvation. We have committed this matter into Your hands and with our faith we see _____ saved, filled with Your Spirit, with a full and clear knowledge of Your Word. Amen — so be it!

Each day after praying this prayer, thank the Lord for this person's salvation. Rejoice and praise God for the victory! Confess the above prayer as done! Thank Him for sending the laborer. Thank Him that Satan is bound. Hallelujah!

Scripture References

Luke 19:10

Matthew 18:18

Matthew 9:38

2 Timothy 2:26 AMP

Job 22:30

45

SPIRIT-CONTROLLED LIFE

The law of the Spirit of life in Christ Jesus has made _____ free from the law of sin and death. His/her life is governed not by the standards and according to the dictates of the flesh but controlled by the Holy Spirit. _____ is not living the life of the flesh. _____ is living the life of the Spirit. The Holy Spirit of God dwells within, and directs and controls him/her.

_____ is a conqueror and gains a surpassing victory through Jesus who loved him/her. _____ does not let himself/herself be overcome by evil, but overcomes and masters evil with good. _____ has on the full armor of light. _____ clothes himself/herself with the Lord Jesus Christ, the Messiah, and makes no provision for indulging the flesh.

_____ is a doer of God's Word. He/she has God's wisdom. He/she is peaceloving, courteous, considerate, gentle, willing to yield to reason, full of compassion and good fruits.

_____ is free from doubts, wavering, and insincerity. He/she is subject to God.

_____ stands firm against the devil. _____ resists the devil and he flees from him/her. _____ comes close to God and God comes close to him/her. _____ does not fear for God never leaves him.

In Christ, _____ is filled with the Godhead: Father, Son, and Holy Spirit. Jesus is his/her Lord!

Scripture References

Romans 8:2,4,9,14,31,37 AMP   James 3:17 AMP
Romans 12:21   Hebrews 13:5
Romans 13:12,14   James 4:7,8
James 1:22   Colossians 2:10

46
RENEW FELLOWSHIP

Father, You hasten Your Word to perform it. I believe and confess that _____ is a disciple of Christ, taught of You, Lord, and obedient to Your will. Great is his/her peace and undisturbed composure. _____ has You in person for his/her teacher. He/she has listened and learned from You and has come to Jesus.

_____ continues to hold to things he/she has learned and of which he/she is convinced. From childhood he/she has had knowledge of and been acquainted with the Word, which is able to instruct him/her and give him/her the understanding of the salvation which comes through faith in Christ Jesus. Father, You will heal _____, lead _____, and recompense _____, and restore comfort to _____.

Jesus gives _____ eternal life. He/she shall never lose it or perish throughout the ages, to all eternity. _____ shall never by any means be destroyed. You, Father, have given _____ to Jesus. You are greater and mightier than all else; no one is able to snatch _____ out of Your hand.

I pray and believe that _____ comes to his/her senses and escapes out of the snare of the devil who has held him/her captive; and that _____ would judge himself/herself.

In the name of Jesus, Satan and every hindering spirit, you are bound in _____ *'s life.*

_____ has become a fellow-heir with Christ, the Messiah, and shares in all He has for him/her and holds the first newborn confidence and original assured expectation firm and unshaken to the end. _____ casts not away his/her confidence for it has great recompense of reward.

Thank You for giving _____ wisdom and revelation — quickening him/her to Your Word. Thank You that _____ enjoys fellowship with You and Jesus and with fellow believers.

Scripture References

Jeremiah 1:12	2 Timothy 2:26 AMP
John 6:45	1 Corinthians 11:31
Isaiah 54:13 AMP	Matthew 18:18
2 Timothy 3:14,15	Hebrews 3:14 AMP
Isaiah 57:18	Hebrews 10:35 AMP
John 10:28,29	Ephesians 1:17
1 John 5:16	1 John 1:3

47
Hedge of protection

Father, in the name of Jesus, we lift up
_____ to You and pray a hedge of protection around him/her. We thank You, Father, that
You are a wall of fire round about _____
and that you set Your angels round about
him/her.

We thank You, Father, that _____
dwells in the secret place of the Most High and
abides under the shadow of the Almighty. We say
of You, Lord, You are his/her refuge and fortress,
in You will he/she trust. You cover _____
with Your feathers, and under Your wings shall
he/she trust. _____ shall not be afraid of
the terror by night or the fiery dart that flies by
day. Only with his/her eyes will _____
behold and see the reward of the wicked.

Because _____ has made You, Lord,
his/her refuge and fortress, no evil shall befall
him/her — no accident will overtake him/her —
neither shall any plague or calamity come near
him/her. For you give Your angels charge over
_____, to keep him/her in all Your ways.

Father, because You have set your love upon
_____, therefore will You deliver him/her.
_____ shall call upon You, and You will
answer him/her. You will be with him/her in
trouble, and will satisfy _____ with long
life and show him/her Your salvation. Not a hair
of his/her head shall perish.

Scripture References

Zechariah 2:5

Psalm 34:7

Psalm 91:1,2 AMP

Psalm 91:4,5 AMP

Psalm 91:8-11 AMP

Psalm 91:14-16 AMP

Luke 21:18

48
EMPLOYMENT

Father, in Jesus' name, we believe and confess Your Word over _____ today knowing that You watch over Your Word to perform it. Your Word prospers in _____ whereto it is sent! Father, You are his/her source of every consolation, comfort, and encouragement. _____ is courageous and grows in strength.

His/her desire is to owe no man anything but to love him. Therefore, _____ is strong and lets not his/her hands be weak or slack, for his/her work shall be rewarded. His/her wages are not counted as a favor or a gift, but as something owed to him. _____ makes it his/her ambition and definitely endeavors to live quietly and peacefully, minds his/her own affairs, and works with his/her hands.

He/she is correct and honorable and commands the respect of the outside world, being self-supporting, dependent on nobody and having need of nothing, for You, Father, supply to the full his/her every need.

He/she works in quietness, earns his/her own food and other necessities. He/she is not weary of doing right and continues in welldoing without weakening. _____ learns to apply himself/herself to good deeds — to honest labor and honorable employment — so that he/she is able to meet necessary demands whenever the occasion may require.

Father, You know the record of his/her works and what he/she is doing. You have set before _____ a door wide open, which no one is able to shut.

_____ does not fear and is not dismayed, for You, Father, strengthen him/her. You, Father, help _____ in Jesus' name, for in Jesus _____ has perfect peace and confidence and is of good cheer, for Jesus overcame the world and deprived it of its power to harm _____. He/she does not fret or have anxiety about anything, for Your peace, Father, mounts guard over his/her heart and mind. _____ knows the secret of facing every situation, for he/she is self-sufficient in Christ's sufficiency. _____ guards his/her mouth and his/her tongue keeping himself/herself from trouble.

_____ prizes Your wisdom, Father, and acknowledges You. You direct, make straight and plain his/her path, and You promote him/her. Therefore, Father, _____ increases in Your wisdom (in broad and full understanding), and in stature and years, and in favor with You, Father, and with man!

Scripture References

Jeremiah 1:12

Isaiah 55:11

2 Corinthians 1:3 AMP

1 Corinthians 16:13

Romans 13:8 AMP

2 Chronicles 15:7 AMP

Romans 4:4 AMP

1 Thessalonians 4:11,12 AMP

2 Thessalonians 3:12,13 AMP

Luke 2:52 AMP

Titus 3:14 AMP

Revelation 3:8 AMP

Isaiah 41:10 AMP

John 16:33 AMP

Philippians 4:6,7 AMP

Philippians 4:12,13 AMP

Proverbs 21:23 AMP

Proverbs 3:6 AMP

Proverbs 4:8

49
PROSPERITY

Father, in the name of Jesus, I praise You with my whole heart. I praise You for Your mighty acts, and according to the abundance of Your greatness! Through faith in the name of Jesus, I say that _____ has received and enjoys life — and has it in abundance — to the full, till it overflows!

Father, according to Your Word, it is Your desire that _____ may prosper and be in health, even as his/her soul prospers. In the name of Jesus, I declare that _____ gets rid of all uncleanness and the rampant outgrowth of wickedness, and in a humble (gentle, modest) spirit receives and welcomes the Word which implanted and rooted [in his/her heart] contains the power to save his/her soul. In the name of Jesus, I affirm that he/she will diligently obey the message; being a doer of the Word, and not merely a listener to it.

I state that his/her delight and desire are in the law of the Lord, and on His law — the precepts, the instructions, the teachings of God — he/she

146

habitually meditates (ponders and studies) by day and by night. Then he/she shall be like a tree firmly planted [and tended] by the streams of water, ready to bring forth his/her fruit in his/her season; his/her leaf also shall not fade or wither, and everything he/she does shall prosper [and come to maturity].

Holy Spirit, Jesus said that You will bring all things to his/her remembrance. Therefore, I decree that he/she will (earnestly) remember the Lord his/her God; for it is You Who gives _____ power to get wealth, that You may establish Your covenant which You swore to our fathers.

Father, I attest that out of the abundance of his/her heart _____ shall say continually, Let the Lord be magnified, Who takes pleasure in the prosperity of His servant. And his/her tongue shall talk of Your righteousness, rightness, and justice, and [his/her reason for] Your praise all the day long.

Scripture References

Psalm 9:1
Psalm 150:2 AMP
John 10:10b AMP
3 John 2
James 1:21,22 AMP

Psalm 1:2,3 AMP
John 14:26b
Deuteronomy 8:18 AMP
Matthew 12:34
Psalm 35:27b,28 AMP

50
FINDING FAVOR
WITH OTHERS

Father, in the name of Jesus, You make Your face to shine upon and enlighten _____ and are gracious (kind, merciful, and giving favor) to him/her. _____ is the head and not the tail. _____ is above only and not beneath.

Thank you for favor for _____ who seeks Your Kingdom and Your righteousness and diligently seeks good. _____ is a blessing to You, Lord, and is a blessing to _____ (name them: family, neighbors, business associates, etc.). Grace (favor) is with _____ who loves the Lord Jesus in sincerity. _____ extends favor, honor, and love to _____ (names). _____ is flowing in Your love, Father. You are pouring out upon _____ the spirit of favor. You crown him/her with glory and honor for he/she is Your child — Your workmanship.

_____ is a success today. _____ is someone very special with You, Lord. _____

148

is growing in the Lord — waxing strong in spirit. Father, You give _____ knowledge and skill in all learning and wisdom.

You bring _____ to find favor, compassion, and loving-kindness with _____ _____ (names). _____ obtains favor in the sight of all who look upon him/her this day in the name of Jesus. _____ is filled with Your fullness — rooted and grounded in love. You are doing exceeding abundantly above all that _____ asks or thinks for Your mighty power is taking over in _____.

Thank you, Father, that _____ is well-favored by You and by man in Jesus' name!

Scripture References

Numbers 6:25
Deuteronomy 28:13
Matthew 6:33
Proverbs 11:27
Ephesians 6:24
Luke 6:38
Zachariah 12:10

Psalm 8:5
Ephesians 2:10
Luke 2:40
Daniel 1:17
Daniel 1:9
Esther 2:15,17
Ephesians 3:19,20

51

IMPROVING COMMUNICATION

_____ is a disciple of Christ — taught of the Lord and obedient to His will. Great is his/her peace and undisturbed composure. _____ is constantly renewed in the spirit of his/her mind — having a fresh mental and spiritual attitude — and is putting on the new nature — the regenerate self — created in God's image, God-like in true righteousness and holiness.

His/her life lovingly expresses truth in all things — speaking truly, dealing truly, living truly. _____ is enfolded in love, growing up in every way and in all things into Him, who is the Head, even Christ, the Messiah, the Anointed One. His/her mouth shall utter truth. _____ speaks excellent and princely things — the opening of his/her lips is for right things. All the words of his/her mouth are righteous. There is nothing contrary to truth or crooked in them.

_____ inclines his/her heart to Your testimonies, Father, and not to covetousness (robbery, sensuality, or unworthy riches).

150

_____ does not love or cherish the world. The love of the Father is in him. _____ is set free from the lust of the flesh (craving for sensual gratification), the lust of the eyes (greedy longings of the mind), and the pride of life (assurance in his own resources or in the stability of earthly things). _____ perceives and knows the truth and that nothing false is of the truth.

_____ prizes Your wisdom, Father, and exalts it, and it will exalt and promote him/her. _____ attends to God's Words; consents and submits to Your sayings. _____ keeps them in the center of his/her heart. For they are life to _____ and medicine to all his/her flesh. _____ keeps his/her heart with all diligence, for out of it flow the springs of life.

_____ will do nothing from factional motives through contentiousness, strife, selfishness, or for unworthy ends — or prompted by conceit and empty arrogance.

Instead, in the true spirit of humility, _____ does regard others as better than himself/herself. _____ esteems and looks upon and is concerned for not merely his/her own interests, but also for the interests of others.

_____ lets this same attitude and purpose and humble mind be in him/her which was in Christ Jesus. Thank You, Father, in Jesus' name.

Scripture References (AMP)

Isaiah 54:13
Ephesians 4:23,24
Ephesians 4:15
Proverbs 8:6-8

Psalm 119:36
1 John 2:15,16,21
Proverbs 4:8,20-23
Philippians 2:2

52

Peace in a Troubled Marriage

Father, in the name of Jesus, we bring _____ before You. We pray and confess Your Word over them, and as we do, we use our faith, believing that Your Word will come to pass.

Therefore we pray and confess that _____ will let all bitterness, indignation, wrath, passion, rage, bad temper, resentment, brawling, clamor, contention, slander, abuse, evil speaking, or blasphemous language be banished from them; also all malice, spite, ill will, or baseness of any kind. We pray that _____ have become useful and helpful and kind to each other, tenderhearted, compassionate, understanding, lovinghearted, forgiving one another readily and freely as You Father, in Christ, forgave them.

Therefore, _____ will be imitators of You, God. They will copy You and follow Your example as well-beloved children imitate their father. _____ will walk in love, esteeming and delighting in one another as Christ loved them and gave Himself up for them, a slain offering and sacrifice to You God, so that it became a sweet fragrance.

Satan, we render you helpless in your activities in the lives of _____. We come against the spirit of separation and divorce, and we loose you from your assignment against them. Satan, your power is broken from their marriage in the name of Jesus.

Father, we thank You that _____ will be constantly renewed in the spirit of their minds having a fresh mental and spiritual attitude. They have put on the new nature and are created in God's image in true righteousness and holiness. They have come to their senses and escaped out of the snare of the devil who has held them captive and henceforth will do Your will, which is that they love one another with the God kind of love, united in total peace and harmony and happiness.

Thank You for the answer, Lord. We know it is done now in the name of Jesus.

Scripture References

Ephesians 4:31,32 AMP

Ephesians 5:1,2

Matthew 18:18

Ephesians 4:23,24

2 Timothy 2:26 AMP

53
SINGLE FEMALE
TRUSTING GOD FOR A MATE

Father, in the name of Jesus, I believe that You are providing Your very best for _____. And the man who will be united with _____ in marriage has awakened to righteousness. Father, as You have rejoiced over Jerusalem, so shall the bridegroom rejoice over _____. Thank You, Father, that he will love _____ as Christ loves the Church. He will nourish, carefully protect, and cherish _____.

Father, I believe, because he is Your best, that doubts, wavering, and insincerity are not a part of him; but he speaks forth the oracles of God, acknowledging Your full counsel with all wisdom and knowledge. He does not speak or act contrary to the Word. He walks totally in love, esteeming and preferring others higher than himself.

Father, I believe that everything not of You shall be removed from _____'s life. And, I thank You for the perfecting of Your Word in her life that she may be thoroughly furnished unto

155

all good works. Father, I praise You for the performance of Your Word in her behalf.

Scripture References

Isaiah 62:5	James 3:17
Ephesians 5:25	Proverbs 8:8

54
SINGLE MALE
TRUSTING GOD FOR A MATE

Father, in the name of Jesus, I believe that You are providing a suitable helpmate for _____. Father, according to Your Word, one who will adapt herself to _____, respect, honor, prefer, and esteem him, stand firmly by his side, united in spirit and purpose, having the same love and being in full accord and of one harmonious mind and intention.

Father, You say in Your Word that a wise, understanding, and prudent wife is from You, and he who finds a true wife finds a good thing and obtains favor of You.

Father, I know that _____ has found favor in Your sight, and I praise You and thank You for Your Word, knowing that You watch over it to perform it.

Scripture References

Ephesians 5:22,33	Proverbs 19:14
Proverbs 18:22	Philippians 2:2

S⁵⁵TUDENT'S
LEARNING ABILITIES

Father, I thank You that You are all the while effectually at work in _____ — energizing and creating in him/her the power and desire — both to will and to work for Your good pleasure and satisfaction and delight.

In the name of Jesus, I thank You that _____ is filled with the full (deep and clear) knowledge of Your will in all spiritual wisdom [that is, in comprehensive insight into Your ways and purposes, Father] and in understanding and discernment of spiritual things; that he/she may walk (live and conduct himself/herself) in a manner worthy of the Lord, fully pleasing to You and desiring to please You in all things, bearing fruit in every good work, and steadily growing and increasing in (and by) the knowledge of God — with fuller, deeper, and clearer insight, acquaintance, and recognition.

I thank You, Father, in the name of Jesus that _____ obeys his/her parents in the Lord [as Your representatives], for this is just and right.

_____ honors (esteems and values as precious) his/her father and mother; that all may be well with him/her and that he/she may live long on the earth.

Thank You, Father, for giving to _____ exceptionally much wisdom and understanding and breadth of mind like the sand of the seashore. He/she is a youth without blemish, well-favored in appearance and skillful in all wisdom, discernment, and understanding, apt in learning knowledge, competent to stand and serve in his/her place of service. God, You have given him/her knowledge and skill in all learning and wisdom. In all matters of wisdom and understanding, he/she is found ten times better than all the [learned].

Thank You, Father, for causing _____ to find favor, good understanding, and high esteem in the sight [or judgment] of God and man. He/she is rooted deep in love and founded securely on love. His/her life lovingly expresses truth in all things — speaking truly, dealing truly, living truly. Enfolded in love, he/she is growing up in every way and in all things unto Him, Who is the Head, [even] Christ, the Messiah, the Anointed One.

Scripture References (AMP)

Philippians 2:13	Daniel 1:4,17a,20
Colossians 1:9,10	Proverbs 3:4
Ephesians 6:1-3	Ephesians 3:17b
1 Kings 4:29	Ephesians 4:15

56

DELIVERANCE FROM HABITS

Father, in the name of Jesus and according to Your Word, I hereby believe in my heart and say with my mouth that Jesus is the Lord of _____'s life. I also confess that from this day forward _____ is set free and delivered from the habit(s) of _____ in the name of Jesus.

Satan you and all your principalities, powers, and master spirits who rule the darkness, and spiritual wickedness in high places are bound up and _____ is loosed from you in the name of Jesus, as it is written in Matthew 18:18-19. No longer can you, Satan, harass or operate any of your unclean spirits or habits over _____. He/she will not become the slave of anything that exalts itself over the Word of God or be brought under its power.

I hereby confess that _____ is strengthened and reinforced with mighty power in his/her innerself by the Holy Spirit who lives and dwells in his/her innermost being. _____ is strong in the Lord. He/she is empowered through his/her union with the Lord.

He/she draws strength from the Lord — that strength which His boundless might provides.

_____ arms himself/herself with the full armor of God, that armor of a heavily armed soldier which God has supplied for him/her...the helmet of salvation...loins girded with truth...breastplate of righteousness...feet shod with the preparation of the gospel of peace...the shield of faith...and the Sword of the Spirit, which is the Word of God. With God's armor on, _____ is able to stand up against all the strategies and deceits and fiery darts of Satan in the name of Jesus.

As an act of his/her will and his/her faith, he/she receives complete and total freedom *now*. He/she is set free and delivered because he/she has called upon the name of the Lord, according to that which is written in His Word.

_____ is able to discipline his/her body and subdue it. He/she is strong. He/she is free. He/she withstands temptation, because Jesus is the Lord of his/her life. Jesus is his/her High Priest, and with Jesus and the Father on his/her side, _____ has the strength for all things. Greater is He that is in _____ than he that is in the world.

Thank You, Lord. I praise You that _____ is whole and redeemed from every

161

evil work. With You and Your Word in _____, he/she controls his/her body. It does not nor can it ever again control him/her in the name of Jesus. Hallelujah!

Scripture References

Romans 10:9,10,13

Matthew 18:18,19

1 Corinthians 6:12

2 Corinthians 10:4,5

Ephesians 3:16 AMP

Ephesians 6:10-17 AMP

Hebrews 4:14-16

1 John 4:4

Romans 8:4,9

Romans 12:21

Romans 13:14

Part II
What the Word Says

Being a mother
WHO IS A GODLY EXAMPLE

He that walketh with wise men shall be wise: but a companion of fools shall be destroyed.

Proverbs 13:20

And he did that which was right in the sight of the Lord, according to all that David his father had done.

2 Chronicles 29:2

But so shall it not be among you: but whosoever will be great among you, shall be your minister:

And whosoever of you will be the chiefest, shall be servant of all.

Mark 10:43,44

For I have given you an example, that ye should do as I have done to you.

Verily, verily, I say unto you, The servant is not greater than his lord; neither he that is sent greater than he that sent him.

A new commandment I give unto you, That ye love one another; as I have loved you, that ye also love one another.

John 13:15,16,34

Now the God of patience and consolation grant you to be likeminded one toward another according to Christ Jesus:

That ye may with one mind and one mouth glorify God, even the Father of our Lord Jesus Christ.

Wherefore receive ye one another, as Christ also received us to the glory of God.

Romans 15:5-7

Servants, be obedient to them that are your masters according to the flesh, with fear and trembling, in singleness of your heart, as unto Christ;

With good will doing service, as to the Lord, and not to men.

Ephesians 6:5,7

Be ye therefore followers of God, as dear children;

And walk in love, as Christ also hath loved us, and hath given himself for us an offering and a sacrifice to God for a sweetsmelling savour.

Ephesians 5:1,2

Hereby perceive we the love of God, because he laid down his life for us: and we ought to lay down our lives for the brethren.

1 John 3:16

Being a Mother
WHO IS LOVING

Though I speak with the tongues of men and of angels, and have not charity, I am become as sounding brass, or a tinkling cymbal.

And though I have the gift of prophecy, and understand all mysteries, and all knowledge; and though I have all faith, so that I could remove mountains, and have not charity, I am nothing.

And though I bestow all my goods to feed the poor, and though I give my body to be burned, and have not charity, it profiteth me nothing.

Charity suffereth long, and is kind; charity envieth not; charity vaunteth not itself, is not puffed up,

Doth not behave itself unseemly, seeketh not her own, is not easily provoked, thinketh no evil;

Rejoiceth not in iniquity, but rejoiceth in the truth;

Beareth all things, believeth all things, hopeth all things, endureth all things.

Charity never faileth.

1 Corinthians 13:1-8a

Hatred stirreth up strifes: but love covereth all sins.

Proverbs 10:12

As the Father hath loved me, so have I loved you: continue ye in my love.

If ye keep my commandments, ye shall abide in my love; even as I have kept my Father's commandments, and abide in his love.

This is my commandment, That ye love one another, as I have loved you.

Greater love hath no man than this, that a man lay down his life for his friends.

Ye are my friends, if ye do whatsoever I command you.

Henceforth I call you not servants; for the servant knoweth not what his lord doeth: but I have called you friends; for all things that I have heard of my Father I have made known unto you.

Ye have not chosen me, but I have chosen you, and ordained you, that ye should go and bring forth fruit, and that your fruit should remain: that whatsoever ye shall ask of the Father in my name, he may give it you.

These things I command you, that ye love one another.

John 15:9,10,12-17

A new commandment I give unto you, That ye love one another; as I have loved you, that ye also love one another.

By this shall all men know that ye are my disciples, if ye have love one to another.

John 13:34,35

Being a mother who gives

Give, and it shall be given unto you; good measure, pressed down, and shaken together, and running over, shall men give into your bosom. For with the same measure that ye mete withal it shall be measured to you again.

Luke 6:38

Be ye strong therefore, and let not your hands be weak: for your work shall be rewarded.

2 Chronicles 15:7

Honour the Lord with thy substance, and with the firstfruits of all thine increase:
So shall thy barns be filled with plenty, and thy presses shall burst out with new wine.

Proverbs 3:9,10

He that hath pity upon the poor lendeth unto the Lord; and that which he hath given will he pay him again.

Proverbs 19:17

Cast thy bread upon the waters: for thou shalt find it after many days.

Ecclesiastes 11:1

He that hath a bountiful eye shall be blessed; for he giveth of his bread to the poor.

Proverbs 22:9

He that giveth unto the poor shall not lack: but he that hideth his eyes shall have many a curse.

Proverbs 28:27

Heal the sick, cleanse the lepers, raise the dead, cast out devils: freely ye have received, freely give.

Matthew 10:8

Upon the first day of the week let every one of you lay by him in store, as God hath prospered him, that there be no gatherings when I come.

1 Corinthians 16:2

Charge them that are rich in this world, that they be not highminded, nor trust in uncertain riches, but in the living God, who giveth us richly all things to enjoy;

That they do good, that they be rich in good works, ready to distribute, willing to communicate;

Laying up in store for themselves a good foundation against the time to come, that they may lay hold on eternal life.

1 Timothy 6:17-19

Beloved, I wish above all things that thou mayest prosper and be in health, even as thy soul prospereth.

3 John 2

BEING A MOTHER
WHO IS DILIGENT

The Lord God is my strength, and he will make my feet like hinds' feet, and he will make me to walk upon mine high places.

Habakkuk 3:19

Be ye strong therefore, and let not your hands be weak: for your work shall be rewarded.

2 Chronicles 15:7

He that gathereth in summer is a wise son: but he that sleepeth in harvest is a son that causeth shame.

Proverbs 10:5

The thoughts of the diligent tend only to plenteousness; but of every one that is hasty only to want.

Proverbs 21:5

The soul of the sluggard desireth, and hath nothing: but the soul of the diligent shall be made fat.

Proverbs 13:4

The hand of the diligent shall bear rule: but the slothful shall be under tribute.

Proverbs 12:24

Seest thou a man diligent in his business? he shall stand before kings; he shall not stand before mean men.

Proverbs 22:29

I can do all things through Christ which strengtheneth me.

Philippians 4:13

As we have therefore opportunity, let us do good unto all men, especially unto them who are of the household of faith.

Galatians 6:10

Now unto him that is able to do exceeding abundantly above all that we ask or think, according to the power that worketh in us.

Ephesians 3:20

And we desire that every one of you do shew the same diligence to the full assurance of hope unto the end.

Hebrews 6:11

Wherefore, beloved, seeing that ye look for such things, be diligent that ye may be found of him in peace, without spot, and blameless.

2 Peter 3:14

BEING A MOTHER
WHO IS RESOURCEFUL

A wise man will hear, and will increase learning; and a man of understanding shall attain unto wise counsels.

Proverbs 1:5

But there is a spirit in man: and the inspiration of the Almighty giveth them understanding.

Job 32:8

I will bless the Lord, who hath given me counsel: my reins also instruct me in the night seasons.

Psalm 16:7

Behold, thou desirest truth in the inward parts: and in the hidden part thou shalt make me to know wisdom.

Psalm 51:6

I will instruct thee and teach thee in the way which thou shalt go: I will guide thee with mine eye.

Psalm 32:8

173

The Lord will perfect that which concerneth me: thy mercy, O Lord, endureth for ever: forsake not the works of thine own hands.

Psalm 138:8

Wisdom is the principal thing; therefore get wisdom: and with all thy getting get understanding.

Exalt her, and she shall promote thee: she shall bring thee to honour, when thou dost embrace her.

Proverbs 4:7,8

Ask, and it shall be given you; seek, and ye shall find; knock, and it shall be opened unto you.

Matthew 7:7

The thoughts of the righteous are right: but the counsels of the wicked are deceit.

Proverbs 12:5

So shall the knowledge of wisdom be unto thy soul: when thou hast found it, then there shall be a reward, and thy expectation shall not be cut off.

Proverbs 24:14

Behold, the former things are come to pass, and new things do I declare: before they spring forth I tell you of them.

Isaiah 42:9

He that walketh with wise men shall be wise: but a companion of fools shall be destroyed.

Proverbs 13:20

BEING A MOTHER
WHO IS UNDERSTANDS

Trust in the Lord with all thine heart; and lean not unto thine own understanding.

In all thy ways acknowledge him, and he shall direct thy paths.

Proverbs 3:5,6

As for God, his way is perfect: the word of the Lord is tried: he is a buckler to all those that trust in him.

Psalm 18:30

Counsel is mine, and sound wisdom: I am understanding; I have strength.

Proverbs 8:14

Teach me thy way, O Lord, and lead me in a plain path, because of mine enemies.

Psalm 27:11

I am thy servant; give me understanding, that I may know thy testimonies.

The entrance of thy words giveth light; it giveth understanding unto the simple.

Let my cry come near before thee, O Lord: give me understanding according to thy word.

Psalm 119:125,130,169

Through wisdom is an house builded; and by understanding it is established:

And by knowledge shall the chambers be filled with all precious and pleasant riches.

Proverbs 24:3,4

For my thoughts are not your thoughts, neither are your ways my ways, saith the Lord.

For as the heavens are higher than the earth, so are my ways higher than your ways, and my thoughts than your thoughts.

Isaiah 55:8,9

Understanding is a wellspring of life unto him that hath it: but the instruction of fools is folly.

The heart of the wise teacheth his mouth, and addeth learning to his lips.

Proverbs 16:22,23

Then opened he their understanding, that they might understand the scriptures.

Luke 24:45

Wherefore be ye not unwise, but understanding what the will of the Lord is.

Ephesians 5:17

Being a mother
WHO LISTENS WELL

But blessed are your eyes, for they see: and your ears, for they hear.

Matthew 13:16

The heart of the prudent getteth knowledge; and the ear of the wise seeketh knowledge.

Proverbs 18:15

And the man said unto me, Son of man, behold with thine eyes, and hear with thine ears, and set thine heart upon all that I shall shew thee.

Ezekiel 40:4a

He that heareth you heareth me; and he that despiseth you despiseth me; and he that despiseth me despiseth him that sent me.

Luke 10:16

Take heed therefore how ye hear: for whosoever hath, to him shall be given; and whosoever hath not, from him shall be taken even that which he seemeth to have.

Luke 8:18

He that is of God heareth God's words: ye therefore hear them not, because ye are not of God.

John 8:47

But be ye doers of the word, and not hearers only, deceiving your own selves.

James 1:22

For if any be a hearer of the word, and not a doer, he is like unto a man beholding his natural face in a glass.

James 1:23

But whoso looketh into the perfect law of liberty, and continueth therein, he being not a forgetful hearer, but a doer of the work, this man shall be blessed in his deed.

James 1:25

He that hath an ear, let him hear what the Spirit saith unto the churches.

Revelation 2:29

Being a Mother
WHO IS COMPASSIONATE

Then shalt thou call, and the Lord shall answer; thou shalt cry, and he shall say, Here I am. If thou take away from the midst of thee the yoke, the putting forth of the finger, and speaking vanity;

And if thou draw out thy soul to the hungry, and satisfy the afflicted soul; then shall thy light rise in obscurity, and thy darkness be as the noon day:

And the Lord shall guide thee continually, and satisfy thy soul in drought, and make fat thy bones: and thou shalt be like a watered garden, and like a spring of water, whose waters fail not.

Isaiah 58:9-11

But he, being full of compassion, forgave their iniquity, and destroyed them not: yea, many a time turned he his anger away, and did not stir up all his wrath.

Psalm 78:38

All the paths of the Lord are mercy and truth unto such as keep his covenant and his testimonies.

Psalm 25:10

The wicked borroweth, and payeth not again: but the righteous sheweth mercy, and giveth.

Psalm 37:21

He that followeth after righteousness and mercy findeth life, righteousness, and honour.

Proverbs 21:21

Can a woman forget her sucking child, that she should not have compassion on the son of her womb? yea, they may forget, yet will I not forget thee.

Isaiah 49:15

And it shall come to pass, after that I have plucked them out I will return, and have compassion on them, and will bring them again, every man to his heritage, and every man to his land.

Jeremiah 12:15

And Jesus, when he came out, saw much people, and was moved with compassion toward them, because they were as sheep not having a shepherd: and he began to teach them many things.

Mark 6:34

IF YOUR DAILY DUTIES
HAVE BECOME BORING

Happy is he that hath the God of Jacob for his help, whose hope is in the Lord his God.

Psalm 146:5

For in thee, O Lord, do I hope: thou wilt hear, O Lord my God.

Psalm 38:15

Why art thou cast down, O my soul? and why art thou disquieted within me? hope in God: for I shall yet praise him, who is the health of my countenance, and my God.

Psalm 43:5

Hope deferred maketh the heart sick: but when the desire cometh, it is a tree of life.

Proverbs 13:12

But I will hope continually, and will yet praise thee more and more.

Psalm 71:14

For which cause we faint not; but though our outward man perish, yet the inward man is renewed day by day.

2 Corinthians 4:16

The glory of this latter house shall be greater than of the former, saith the Lord of hosts: and in this place will I give peace, saith the Lord of hosts.

Haggai 2:9

Now the God of hope fill you with all joy and peace in believing, that ye may abound in hope, through the power of the Holy Ghost.

Romans 15:13

And God is able to make all grace abound toward you; that ye, always having all sufficiency in all things, may abound to every good work.

2 Corinthians 9:8

And let us not be weary in well doing: for in due season we shall reap, if we faint not.

Galatians 6:9

That he would grant you, according to the riches of his glory, to be strengthened with might by his Spirit in the inner man.

Ephesians 3:16

And the peace of God, which passeth all understanding, shall keep your hearts and minds through Christ Jesus.

Philippians 4:7

BEING A MOTHER WHO BALANCES FAMILY AND CAREER

But if any provide not for his own, and specially for those of his own house, he hath denied the faith, and is worse than an infidel.

1 Timothy 5:8

One that ruleth well his own house, having his children in subjection with all gravity;

For if a man know not how to rule his own house, how shall he take care of the church of God?

1 Timothy 3:4,5

Moreover I will establish his kingdom for ever, if he be constant to do my commandments and my judgments, as at this day.

1 Chronicles 28:7

Only take heed to thyself, and keep thy soul diligently, lest thou forget the things which thine eyes have seen, and lest they depart from thy heart all the days of thy life: but teach them thy sons, and thy sons' sons.

Deuteronomy 4:9

Blessed is every one that feareth the Lord; that walketh in his ways.

For thou shalt eat the labour of thine hands: happy shalt thou be, and it shall be well with thee.

Thy wife shall be as a fruitful vine by the sides of thine house: thy children like olive plants round about thy table.

Behold, that thus shall the man be blessed that feareth the Lord.

Psalm 128:1-4

The soul of the sluggard desireth, and hath nothing: but the soul of the diligent shall be made fat.

Proverbs 13:4

A man's heart deviseth his way: but the Lord directeth his steps.

Proverbs 16:9

Correct thy son, and he shall give thee rest; yea, he shall give delight unto thy soul.

Proverbs 29:17

The just man walketh in his integrity: his children are blessed after him.

Proverbs 20:7

Through wisdom is an house builded; and by understanding it is established.

Proverbs 24:3

Train up a child in the way he should go: and when he is old, he will not depart from it.

Proverbs 22:6

IF YOU ARE THE SOLE PROVIDER FOR THE FAMILY

Through wisdom is an house builded; and by understanding it is established.

Proverbs 24:3

But seek ye first the kingdom of God, and his righteousness; and all these things shall be added unto you.

Matthew 6:33

But my God shall supply all your need according to his riches in glory by Christ Jesus.

Philippians 4:19

The Lord is good, a strong hold in the day of trouble; and he knoweth them that trust in him.

Nahum 1:7

For thou art my rock and my fortress; therefore for thy name's sake lead me, and guide me.

Psalm 31:3

I will instruct thee and teach thee in the way which thou shalt go: I will guide thee with mine eye.

Psalm 32:8

Trust in the Lord with all thine heart; and lean not unto thine own understanding.

Proverbs 3:5

For the Lord giveth wisdom: out of his mouth cometh knowledge and understanding.

Proverbs 2:6

Thou shalt guide me with thy counsel, and afterward receive me to glory.

Psalm 73:24

He becometh poor that dealeth with a slack hand: but the hand of the diligent maketh rich.

Proverbs 10:4

The hand of the diligent shall bear rule: but the slothful shall be under tribute.

Proverbs 12:24

The soul of the sluggard desireth, and hath nothing: but the soul of the diligent shall be made fat.

Proverbs 13:4

Love not sleep, lest thou come to poverty; open thine eyes, and thou shalt be satisfied with bread.

Proverbs 20:13

Seest thou a man diligent in his business? he shall stand before kings; he shall not stand before mean men.

Proverbs 22:29

IF YOU FEEL DEPRIVED
OF YOUR TIME ALONE

The steps of a good man are ordered by the Lord: and he delighteth in his way.

Psalm 37:23

I have set the Lord always before me: because he is at my right hand, I shall not be moved.

Therefore my heart is glad, and my glory rejoiceth: my flesh also shall rest in hope.

Psalm 16:8

Thy testimonies also are my delight and my counsellors.

Psalm 119:24

Casting down imaginations, and every high thing that exalteth itself against the knowledge of God, and bringing into captivity every thought to the obedience of Christ.

2 Corinthians 10:5

I beseech you therefore, brethren, by the mercies of God, that ye present your bodies a living sacrifice, holy, acceptable unto God, which is your reasonable service.

And be not conformed to this world: but be ye transformed by the renewing of your mind, that ye may prove what is that good, and acceptable, and perfect, will of God.

Be kindly affectioned one to another with brotherly love; in honour preferring one another;

Not slothful in business; fervent in spirit; serving the Lord;

Rejoicing in hope; patient in tribulation; continuing instant in prayer;

Distributing to the necessity of saints; given to hospitality.

Romans 12:1,2,10-13

Looking diligently lest any man fail of the grace of God; lest any root of bitterness springing up trouble you, and thereby many be defiled.

Hebrews 12:15

Finally, my brethren, be strong in the Lord, and in the power of his might.

Ephesians 6:10

Be careful for nothing; but in every thing by prayer and supplication with thanksgiving let your requests be made known unto God.

And the peace of God, which passeth all understanding, shall keep your hearts and minds through Christ Jesus.

I can do all things through Christ which strengtheneth me.

Philippians 4:6,7,13

IF YOU NEED STRENGTH

I can do all things through Christ which strengtheneth me.

Philippians 4:13

The Lord God is my strength, and he will make my feet like hinds' feet, and he will make me to walk upon mine high places.

Habakkuk 3:19

For the joy of the Lord is your strength.

Nehemiah 8:10b

The Lord is my light and my salvation; whom shall I fear? the Lord is the strength of my life; of whom shall I be afraid?

Wait on the Lord: be of good courage, and he shall strengthen thine heart: wait, I say, on the Lord.

Psalm 27:1,14

The Lord is my rock, and my fortress, and my deliverer; my God, my strength, in whom I will trust; my buckler, and the horn of my salvation, and my high tower.

Psalm 18:2

Be of good courage, and he shall strengthen your heart, all ye that hope in the Lord.

Psalm 31:24

The way of the Lord is strength to the upright: but destruction shall be to the workers of iniquity.

Proverbs 10:29

In the day when I cried thou answeredst me, and strengthenedst me with strength in my soul.

Psalm 138:3

Counsel is mine, and sound wisdom: I am understanding; I have strength.

Proverbs 8:14

In the fear of the Lord is strong confidence: and his children shall have a place of refuge.

Proverbs 14:26

Behold, God is my salvation; I will trust, and not be afraid: for the Lord Jehovah is my strength and my song; he also is become my salvation.

Isaiah 12:2

For thus saith the Lord God, the Holy One of Israel; In returning and rest shall ye be saved; in quietness and in confidence shall be your strength: and ye would not.

Isaiah 30:15

A wise man is strong; yea, a man of knowledge increaseth strength.

Proverbs 24:5

IF YOU NEED PEACE WITHIN

Therefore being justified by faith, we have peace with God through our Lord Jesus Christ.
Romans 5:1

I will both lay me down in peace, and sleep: for thou, Lord, only makest me dwell in safety.
Psalm 4:8

But the meek shall inherit the earth; and shall delight themselves in the abundance of peace.
Mark the perfect man, and behold the upright: for the end of that man is peace.
Psalm 37:11,37

Great peace have they which love thy law: and nothing shall offend them.
Psalm 119:165

For ye shall go out with joy, and be led forth with peace: the mountains and the hills shall break forth before you into singing, and all the trees of the field shall clap their hands.
Isaiah 55:12

Thou wilt keep him in perfect peace, whose mind is stayed on thee: because he trusteth in thee.

Lord, thou wilt ordain peace for us: for thou also hast wrought all our works in us.

Isaiah 26:3,12

He shall enter into peace: they shall rest in their beds, each one walking in his uprightness.

Isaiah 57:2

Peace I leave with you, my peace I give unto you: not as the world giveth, give I unto you. Let not your heart be troubled, neither let it be afraid.

John 14:27

For to be carnally minded is death; but to be spiritually minded is life and peace.

Romans 8:6

Grace be to you and peace from God the Father, and from our Lord Jesus Christ.

Galatians 1:3

Be careful for nothing; but in every thing by prayer and supplication with thanksgiving let your requests be made known unto God.

And the peace of God, which passeth all understanding, shall keep your hearts and minds through Christ Jesus.

Those things, which ye have both learned, and received, and heard, and seen in me, do: and the God of peace shall be with you.

Philippians 4:6,7,9

But the fruit of the Spirit is love, joy, peace, longsuffering, gentleness, goodness, faith.

Galatians 5:22

IF YOU NEED TO FORGIVE

Then came Peter to him, and said, Lord, how oft shall my brother sin against me, and I forgive him? till seven times?

Jesus saith unto him, ''I say not unto thee, Until seven times: but, Until seventy times seven.''

Matthew 18:21,22

But I say unto you, That ye resist not evil: but whosoever shall smite thee on thy right cheek, turn to him the other also.

Matthew 5:39

The discretion of a man deferreth his anger; and it is his glory to pass over a transgression.

Proverbs 19:11

If thine enemy be hungry, give him bread to eat; and if he be thirsty, give him water to drink.

Proverbs 25:21

Rejoice not when thine enemy falleth, and let not thine heart be glad when he stumbleth:

Say not, I will do so to him as he hath done to me: I will render to the man according to his work.

Proverbs 24:17,29

Blessed are the merciful: for they shall obtain mercy.

Matthew 5:7

But I say unto you, Love your enemies, bless them that curse you, do good to them that hate you, and pray for them which despitefully use you, and persecute you.

Matthew 5:44

And forgive us our debts, as we forgive our debtors.

For if ye forgive men their trespasses, your heavenly Father will also forgive you:

But if ye forgive not men their trespasses, neither will your Father forgive your trespasses.

Matthew 6:12,14,15

Take heed to yourselves: If thy brother trespass against thee, rebuke him; and if he repent, forgive him.

And if he trespass against thee seven times in a day, and seven times in a day turn again to thee, saying, I repent; thou shalt forgive him.

Luke 17:3,4

And when ye stand praying, forgive, if ye have ought against any: that your Father also which is in heaven may forgive you your trespasses.

Mark 11:25

194

IF YOU NEED FAITH

Fear not, O land; be glad and rejoice: for the Lord will do great things.

Joel 2:21

The Lord is my shepherd; I shall not want.

Psalm 23:1

So then faith cometh by hearing, and hearing by the word of God.

Romans 10:17

But what saith it? The word is nigh thee, even in thy mouth, and in thy heart: that is, the word of faith, which we preach.

Romans 10:8

The Lord also will be a refuge for the oppressed, a refuge in times of trouble.

And they that know thy name will put their trust in thee: for thou, Lord, hast not forsaken them that seek thee.

Psalm 9:9,10

But let all those that put their trust in thee rejoice: let them ever shout for joy, because thou defendest them: let them also that love thy name be joyful in thee.

Psalm 5:11

It is better to trust in the Lord than to put confidence in man.

It is better to trust in the Lord than to put confidence in princes.

Psalm 118:8,9

Now the God of hope fill you with all joy and peace in believing, that ye may abound in hope, through the power of the Holy Ghost.

Romans 15:13

For whatsoever is born of God overcometh the world: and this is the victory that overcometh the world, even our faith.

1 John 5:4

Now the just shall live by faith: but if any man draw back, my soul shall have no pleasure in him.

But we are not of them who draw back unto perdition; but of them that believe to the saving of the soul.

Hebrews 10:38,39

And David said to Solomon his son, Be strong and of good courage, and do it: fear not, nor be dismayed: for the Lord God, even my God, will be with thee; he will not fail thee, nor forsake thee, until thou hast finished all the work for the service of the house of the Lord.

I Chronicles 28:20

IF YOU NEED JOY

Make a joyful noise unto the Lord, all ye lands.
Serve the Lord with gladness: come before his presence with singing.

Psalm 100:1,2

Thou wilt shew me the path of life: in thy presence is fulness of joy; at thy right hand there are pleasures for evermore.

Psalm 16:11

I will be glad and rejoice in thee: I will sing praise to thy name, O thou most High.

Psalm 9:2

Glory and honour are in his presence; strength and gladness are in his place.

1 Chronicles 16:27

The statutes of the Lord are right, rejoicing the heart: the commandment of the Lord is pure, enlightening the eyes.

Psalm 19:8

And my soul shall be joyful in the Lord: it shall rejoice in his salvation.

Psalm 35:9

The Lord is my strength and my shield; my heart trusted in him, and I am helped: therefore my heart greatly rejoiceth; and with my song will I praise him.

Psalm 28:7

Blessed is the people that know the joyful sound: they shall walk, O Lord, in the light of thy countenance.

In thy name shall they rejoice all the day: and in thy righteousness shall they be exalted.

Psalm 89:15,16

These things have I spoken unto you, that my joy might remain in you, and that your joy might be full.

John 15:11

Notwithstanding in this rejoice not, that the spirits are subject unto you; but rather rejoice, because your names are written in heaven.

Luke 10:20

For ye were sometimes darkness, but now are ye light in the Lord: walk as children of light.

Ephesians 5:8

Thou hast made known to me the ways of life; thou shalt make me full of joy with thy countenance.

Acts 2:28

And the disciples were filled with joy, and with the Holy Ghost.

Acts 13:52

IF YOU NEED MOTIVATION

And that ye study to be quiet, and to do your own business, and to work with your own hands, as we commanded you;

That ye may walk honestly toward them that are without, and that ye may have lack of nothing.

1 Thessalonians 4:11,12

Servants, obey in all things your masters according to the flesh; not with eyeservice, as menpleasers; but in singleness of heart, fearing God:

And whatsoever ye do, do it heartily, as to the Lord, and not unto men.

Colossians 3:22,23

Seest thou a man diligent in his business? he shall stand before kings; he shall not stand before mean men.

Proverbs 22:29

Wherefore I put thee in remembrance that thou stir up the gift of God, which is in thee by the putting on of my hands.

For God hath not given us the spirit of fear; but of power, and of love, and of a sound mind.

2 Timothy 1:6,7

I lead in the way of righteousness, in the midst of the paths of judgment:

That I may cause those that love me to inherit substance; and I will fill their treasures.

Proverbs 8:20,21

He that tilleth his land shall be satisfied with bread: but he that followeth vain persons is void of understanding.

Proverbs 12:11

He that gathereth in summer is a wise son: but he that sleepeth in harvest is a son that causeth shame.

Proverbs 10:5

For even when we were with you, this we commanded you, that if any would not work, neither should he eat.

2 Thessalonians 3:10

Love not sleep, lest thou come to poverty; open thine eyes, and thou shalt be satisfied with bread.

Proverbs 20:13

Nay, in all these things we are more than conquerors through him that loved us.

Romans 8:37

IF YOU NEED PATIENCE

In your patience possess ye your souls.
Luke 21:19

Rest in the Lord, and wait patiently for him: fret not thyself because of him who prospereth in his way, because of the man who bringeth wicked devices to pass.

Cease from anger, and forsake wrath: fret not thyself in any wise to do evil.

For evildoers shall be cut off: but those that wait upon the Lord, they shall inherit the earth.
Psalm 37:7-9

That ye might walk worthy of the Lord unto all pleasing, being fruitful in every good work, and increasing in the knowledge of God;

Strengthened with all might, according to his glorious power, unto all patience and longsuffering with joyfulness.
Colossians 1:10,11

Better is the end of a thing than the beginning thereof: and the patient in spirit is better than the proud in spirit.

Be not hasty in thy spirit to be angry: for anger resteth in the bosom of fools.

Ecclesiastes 7:8,9

With all lowliness and meekness, with longsuffering, forbearing one another in love.

Ephesians 4:2

But thou, O man of God, flee these things; and follow after righteousness, godliness, faith, love, patience, meekness.

1 Timothy 6:11

Now we exhort you, brethren, warn them that are unruly, comfort the feebleminded, support the weak, be patient toward all men.

1 Thessalonians 5:14

For ye have need of patience, that, after ye have done the will of God, ye might receive the promise.

Hebrews 10:36

That ye be not slothful, but followers of them who through faith and patience inherit the promises.

Hebrews 6:12

And so, after he had patiently endured, he obtained the promise.

Hebrews 6:15

IF YOU FEEL INADEQUATE

It is better to trust in the Lord than to put confidence in man.

Psalm 118:8

For the Lord thy God is a merciful God; he will not forsake thee, neither destroy thee, nor forget the covenant of thy fathers which he sware unto them.

Deuteronomy 4:31

Though an host should encamp against me, my heart shall not fear: though war should rise against me, in this will I be confident.

For in the time of trouble he shall hide me in his pavilion: in the secret of his tabernacle shall he hide me; he shall set me up upon a rock.

Psalm 27:3,5

But thou, O Lord, art a shield for me; my glory, and the lifter up of mine head.

Psalm 3:3

My voice shalt thou hear in the morning, O Lord; in the morning will I direct my prayer unto thee, and will look up.

Psalm 5:3

He giveth power to the faint; and to them that have no might he increaseth strength.

But they that wait upon the Lord shall renew their strength; they shall mount up with wings as eagles; they shall run, and not be weary; and they shall walk, and not faint.

Isaiah 40:29,31

Fear thou not; for I am with thee: be not dismayed; for I am thy God: I will strengthen thee; yea, I will help thee; yea, I will uphold thee with the right hand of my righteousness.

Isaiah 41:10

I will not leave you comfortless: I will come to you.

John 14:18

Wherein ye greatly rejoice, though now for a season, if need be, ye are in heaviness through manifold temptations:

That the trial of your faith, being much more precious than of gold that perisheth, though it be tried with fire, might be found unto praise and honour and glory at the appearing of Jesus Christ:

Whom having not seen, ye love; in whom, though now ye see him not, yet believing, ye rejoice with joy unspeakable and full of glory:

Receiving the end of your faith, even the salvation of your souls.

1 Peter 1:6-9

IF YOU ARE
UNDER UNUSUAL STRESS

Rejoicing in hope; patient in tribulation; continuing instant in prayer.

Romans 12:12

Persecuted, but not forsaken; cast down, but not destroyed.

2 Corinthians 4:9

Who shall separate us from the love of Christ? shall tribulation, or distress, or persecution, or famine, or nakedness, or peril, or sword?

Romans 8:35

And not only so, but we glory in tribulations also: knowing that tribulation worketh patience.

Romans 5:3

Who comforteth us in all our tribulation, that we may be able to comfort them which are in any trouble, by the comfort wherewith we ourselves are comforted of God.

2 Corinthians 1:4

These things I have spoken unto you, that in me ye might have peace. In the world ye shall have tribulation: but be of good cheer; I have overcome the world.

John 16:33

That the trial of your faith, being much more precious than of gold that perisheth, though it be tried with fire, might be found unto praise and honour and glory at the appearing of Jesus Christ.

1 Peter 1:7

But and if ye suffer for righteousness' sake, happy are ye: and be not afraid of their terror, neither be troubled.

1 Peter 3:14

In the day of my trouble I will call upon thee: for thou wilt answer me.

Psalm 86:7

For which cause we faint not; but though our outward man perish, yet the inward man is renewed day by day.

2 Corinthians 4:16

The righteous is delivered out of trouble, and the wicked cometh in his stead.

Proverbs 11:8

In my distress I cried unto the Lord, and he heard me.

Psalm 120:1

Be careful for nothing; but in every thing by prayer and supplication with thanksgiving let your requests be made known unto God.

Philippians 4:6

IF YOU NEED PROTECTION

God is our refuge and strength, a very present help in trouble.

Therefore will not we fear, though the earth be removed, and though the mountains be carried into the midst of the sea.

Psalm 46:1,2

He that dwelleth in the secret place of the most High shall abide under the shadow of the Almighty.

I will say of the Lord, He is my refuge and my fortress: my God; in him will I trust.

Surely he shall deliver thee from the snare of the fowler, and from the noisome pestilence.

He shall cover thee with his feathers, and under his wings shalt thou trust: his truth shall be thy shield and buckler.

Thou shalt not be afraid for the terror by night; nor for the arrow that flieth by day;

Nor for the pestilence that walketh in darkness; nor for the destruction that wasteth at noonday.

A thousand shall fall at thy side, and ten thousand at thy right hand; but it shall not come nigh thee.

Only with thine eyes shalt thou behold and see the reward of the wicked.

Because thou hast made the Lord, which is my refuge, even the most High, thy habitation;

There shall no evil befall thee, neither shall any plague come nigh thy dwelling.

For he shall give his angels charge over thee, to keep thee in all thy ways.

They shall bear thee up in their hands, lest thou dash thy foot against a stone.

Thou shalt tread upon the lion and adder: the young lion and the dragon shalt thou trample under feet.

Because he hath set his love upon me, therefore will I deliver him: I will set him on high, because he hath known my name.

He shall call upon me, and I will answer him: I will be with him in trouble; I will deliver him, and honour him.

With long life will I satisfy him, and shew him my salvation.

Psalm 91:1-16

For I, saith the Lord, will be unto her a wall of fire round about, and will be the glory in the midst of her.

Zechariah 2:5

IF YOU ARE
FACING SEXUAL TEMPTATION

And lead us not into temptation, but deliver us from evil: For thine is the kingdom, and the power, and the glory, for ever. Amen.

Matthew 6:13

Watch and pray, that ye enter not into temptation: the spirit indeed is willing, but the flesh is weak.

Matthew 26:41

The Lord knoweth how to deliver the godly out of temptations, and to reserve the unjust unto the day of judgment to be punished:

2 Peter 2:9

But thou, O Lord, art a shield for me; my glory, and the lifter up of mine head.

Psalm 3:3

Be pleased, O Lord, to deliver me: O Lord, make haste to help me.

Let them be ashamed and confounded together that seek after my soul to destroy it; let them be driven backward and put to shame that wish me evil.

Psalm 40:13,14

Thy word have I hid in mine heart, that I might not sin against thee.

Psalm 119:11

For the Lord shall be thy confidence, and shall keep thy foot from being taken.

Proverbs 3:26

In the fear of the Lord is strong confidence: and his children shall have a place of refuge.

Proverbs 14:26

Let thine eyes look right on, and let thine eyelids look straight before thee.

Turn not to the right hand nor to the left: remove thy foot from evil.

Proverbs 4:25,27

The way of the Lord is strength to the upright: but destruction shall be to the workers of iniquity.

Proverbs 10:29

He that covereth his sins shall not prosper: but whoso confesseth and forsaketh them shall have mercy.

Proverbs 28:13

Fear thou not; for I am with thee: be not dismayed; for I am thy God: I will strengthen thee; yea, I will help thee; yea, I will uphold thee with the right hand of my righteousness.

Isaiah 41:10

IF YOU ARE ANGRY OR RESENTFUL

He that is slow to anger is better than the mighty; and he that ruleth his spirit than he that taketh a city.

Proverbs 16:32

Blessed are the peacemakers: for they shall be called the children of God.

Matthew 5:9

Cease from anger, and forsake wrath: fret not thyself in any wise to do evil.

Psalm 37:8

Trust in the Lord with all thine heart; and lean not unto thine own understanding.

In all thy ways acknowledge him, and he shall direct thy paths.

For the Lord shall be thy confidence.

Proverbs 3:5,6,26a

Behold, thou desirest truth in the inward parts: and in the hidden part thou shalt make me to know wisdom.

Create in me a clean heart, O God; and renew a right spirit within me.

Psalm 51:6,10

In God I will praise his word, in God I have put my trust; I will not fear what flesh can do unto me.

Psalm 56:4

Teach me thy way, O Lord; I will walk in thy truth: unite my heart to fear thy name.

Psalm 86:11

He that is soon angry dealeth foolishly: and a man of wicked devices is hated.

Proverbs 14:17

Behold, God is my salvation; I will trust, and not be afraid: for the Lord Jehovah is my strength and my song; he also is become my salvation.

Isaiah 12:2

Be not hasty in thy spirit to be angry: for anger resteth in the bosom of fools.

Ecclesiastes 7:9

But the fruit of the Spirit is love, joy, peace, longsuffering, gentleness, goodness, faith,
Meekness, temperance: against such there is no law.

Galatians 5:22,23

Finally, brethren, whatsoever things are true, whatsoever things are honest, whatsoever things are just, whatsoever things are pure, whatsoever things are lovely, whatsoever things are of good report; if there be any virtue, and if there be any praise, think on these things.

Philippians 4:8

IF YOU FEEL LONELY
AND UNAPRECIATED

What shall we then say to these things? If God be for us, who can be against us?

Romans 8:31

Be strong and of a good courage, fear not, nor be afraid of them: for the Lord thy God, he it is that doth go with thee; he will not fail thee, nor forsake thee.

Deuteronomy 31:6

And they that know thy name will put their trust in thee: for thou, Lord, hast not forsaken them that seek thee.

Psalm 9:10

My soul, wait thou only upon God; for my expectation is from him.

Psalm 62:5

Yea, though I walk through the valley of the shadow of death, I will fear no evil: for thou art with me; thy rod and thy staff they comfort me.

Psalm 23:4

Why art thou cast down, O my soul? and why art thou disquieted within me? hope in God: for I shall yet praise him, who is the health of my countenance, and my God.

Psalm 43:5

Trust in the Lord with all thine heart; and lean not unto thine own understanding.

In all thy ways acknowledge him, and he shall direct thy paths.

Proverbs 3:5,6

I wait for the Lord, my soul doth wait, and in his word do I hope.

Psalm 130:5

Fear thou not; for I am with thee: be not dismayed; for I am thy God: I will strengthen thee; yea, I will help thee; yea, I will uphold thee with the right hand of my righteousness.

Isaiah 41:10

Teaching them to observe all things whatsoever I have commanded you: and, lo, I am with you alway, even unto the end of the world. Amen.

Matthew 28:20

So that we may boldly say, The Lord is my helper, and I will not fear what man shall do unto me.

Hebrews 13:6

Casting all your care upon him; for he careth for you.

1 Peter 5:7

IF YOU ARE HAVING DOUBTS

And he said, Lord, I believe. And he worshipped him.

John 9:38

The other disciples therefore said unto him, We have seen the Lord. But he said unto them, Except I shall see in his hands the print of the nails, and put my finger into the print of the nails, and thrust my hand into his side, I will not believe.

And after eight days again his disciples were within, and Thomas with them: then came Jesus, the doors being shut, and stood in the midst, and said, Peace be unto you.

Then saith he to Thomas, Reach hither thy finger, and behold my hands; and reach hither thy hand, and thrust it into my side: and be not faithless, but believing.

And Thomas answered and said unto him, My Lord and my God.

Jesus saith unto him, Thomas, because thou hast seen me, thou hast believed: blessed are they that have not seen, and yet have believed.

And many other signs truly did Jesus in the presence of his disciples, which are not written in this book:

But these are written, that ye might believe that Jesus is the Christ, the Son of God; and that believing ye might have life through his name.

John 20:25-31

As soon as Jesus heard the word that was spoken, he saith unto the ruler of the synagogue, Be not afraid, only believe.

Mark 5:36

Jesus said unto him, If thou canst believe, all things are possible to him that believeth.

And straightway the father of the child cried out, and said with tears, Lord, I believe; help thou mine unbelief.

Mark 9:23,24

For verily I say unto you, That whosoever shall say unto this mountain, Be thou removed, and be thou cast into the sea; and shall not doubt in his heart, but shall believe that those things which he saith shall come to pass; he shall have whatsoever he saith.

Therefore I say unto you, What things soever ye desire, when ye pray, believe that ye receive them, and ye shall have them.

Mark 11:23,24

IF YOUR CHILD IS REBELLIOUS TOWARD YOU

Behold, I give unto you power to tread on serpents and scorpions, and over all the power of the enemy: and nothing shall by any means hurt you.

Luke 10:19

Train up a child in the way he should go: and when he is old, he will not depart from it.

Proverbs 22:6

Shew me thy ways, O Lord; teach me thy paths.

What man is he that feareth the Lord? him shall he teach in the way that he shall choose.

Psalm 25:4,12

Answer not a fool according to his folly, lest thou also be like unto him.

Proverbs 26:4

The Lord is my strength and my shield; my heart trusted in him, and I am helped: therefore my heart greatly rejoiceth; and with my song will I praise him.

Psalm 28:7

217

Though I walk in the midst of trouble, thou wilt revive me: thou shalt stretch forth thine hand against the wrath of mine enemies, and thy right hand shall save me.

Psalm 138:7

Teach me to do thy will; for thou art my God: thy spirit is good; lead me into the land of uprightness.

Psalm 143:10

Cast thy burden upon the Lord, and he shall sustain thee: he shall never suffer the righteous to be moved.

Psalm 55:22

If ye be willing and obedient, ye shall eat the good of the land:

But if ye refuse and rebel, ye shall be devoured with the sword: for the mouth of the Lord hath spoken it.

Isaiah 1:19,20

Can a woman forget her sucking child, that she should not have compassion on the son of her womb? yea, they may forget, yet will I not forget thee.

Isaiah 49:15

And I will give unto thee the keys of the kingdom of heaven: and whatsoever thou shalt bind on earth shall be bound in heaven: and whatsoever thou shalt loose on earth shall be loosed in heaven.

Matthew 16:19

IF YOUR CHILD IS REBELLIOUS TOWARD GOD

Train up a child in the way he should go: and when he is old, he will not depart from it.

Proverbs 22:6

Wait on the Lord: be of good courage, and he shall strengthen thine heart: wait, I say, on the Lord.

Psalm 27:14

Our soul waiteth for the Lord: he is our help and our shield.

Psalm 33:20

Cast thy burden upon the Lord, and he shall sustain thee: he shall never suffer the righteous to be moved.

Psalm 55:22

Correct thy son, and he shall give thee rest; yea, he shall give delight unto thy soul.

Proverbs 29:17

I wait for the Lord, my soul doth wait, and in his word do I hope.

Psalm 130:5

The Lord will perfect that which concerneth me: thy mercy, O Lord, endureth for ever: forsake not the works of thine own hands.

Psalm 138:8

For the Lord will not cast off his people, neither will he forsake his inheritance.

Psalm 94:14

Fear thou not; for I am with thee: be not dismayed; for I am thy God: I will strengthen thee; yea, I will help thee; yea, I will uphold thee with the right hand of my righteousness.

Isaiah 41:10

And all thy children shall be taught of the Lord; and great shall be the peace of thy children.

Isaiah 54:13

Let us hold fast the profession of our faith without wavering; for he is faithful that promised.

Hebrews 10:23

That the trial of your faith, being much more precious than of gold that perisheth, though it be tried with fire, might be found unto praise and honour and glory at the appearing of Jesus Christ:

1 Peter 1:7

Casting all your care upon him; for he careth for you.

1 Peter 5:7

IF YOUR CHILD IS UNFORGIVING

I will instruct thee and teach thee in the way which thou shalt go: I will guide thee with mine eye.

Psalm 32:8

Great peace have they which love thy law: and nothing shall offend them.

Psalm 119:165

Unless the Lord had been my help, my soul had almost dwelt in silence.
When I said, My foot slippeth; thy mercy, O Lord, held me up.

Psalm 94:17,18

Cast thy burden upon the Lord, and he shall sustain thee: he shall never suffer the righteous to be moved.

Psalm 55:22

Give instruction to a wise man, and he will be yet wiser: teach a just man, and he will increase in learning.

Proverbs 9:9

Open rebuke is better than secret love.

Proverbs 27:5

Quicken me, O Lord, for thy name's sake: for thy righteousness' sake bring my soul out of trouble.

Psalm 143:11

Finally, my brethren, be strong in the Lord, and in the power of his might.

Ephesians 6:10

For the Lord God will help me; therefore shall I not be confounded.

Isaiah 50:7a

That he would grant you, according to the riches of his glory, to be strengthened with might by his Spirit in the inner man.

Ephesians 3:16

And above all these things put on charity, which is the bond of perfectness.

And whatsoever ye do in word or deed, do all in the name of the Lord Jesus, giving thanks to God and the Father by him.

Colossians 3:14,17

If any of you lack wisdom, let him ask of God, that giveth to all men liberally, and upbraideth not; and it shall be given him.

James 1:5

IF YOUR CHILD IS WITHDRAWING FROM YOU

Now faith is the substance of things hoped for, the evidence of things not seen.

For by it the elders obtained a good report.

Through faith we understand that the worlds were framed by the word of God, so that things which are seen were not made of things which do appear.

Hebrews 11:1-3

Commit thy works unto the Lord, and thy thoughts shall be established.

Proverbs 16:3

And he shall turn the heart of the fathers to the children, and the heart of the children to their fathers, lest I come and smite the earth with a curse.

Malachi 4:6

Even every one that is called by my name: for I have created him for my glory, I have formed him; yea, I have made him.

This people have I formed for myself; they shall shew forth my praise.

Isaiah 43:7,21

And they that be wise shall shine as the brightness of the firmament; and they that turn many to righteousness as the stars for ever and ever.

Daniel 12:3

Be of good courage, and he shall strengthen your heart, all ye that hope in the Lord.

Psalm 31:24

Ye are the salt of the earth: but if the salt have lost his savour, wherewith shall it be salted?

Matthew 5:13a

And when ye stand praying, forgive, if ye have ought against any: that your Father also which is in heaven may forgive you your trespasses.

But if ye do not forgive, neither will your Father which is in heaven forgive your trespasses.

Mark 11:25,26

Why art thou cast down, O my soul? and why art thou disquieted within me? hope in God: for I shall yet praise him, who is the health of my countenance, and my God.

Psalm 43:5

IF YOUR CHILD SUFFERS PERSONAL FAILURE OR LOSS

But they that wait upon the Lord shall renew their strength; they shall mount up with wings as eagles; they shall run, and not be weary; and they shall walk, and not faint.

Isaiah 40:31

For thus saith the Lord God, the Holy One of Israel; In returning and rest shall ye be saved; in quietness and in confidence shall be your strength: and ye would not.

Isaiah 30:15

He maketh me to lie down in green pastures: he leadeth me beside the still waters.

He restoreth my soul: he leadeth me in the paths of righteousness for his name's sake.

Psalm 23:2,3

Let integrity and uprightness preserve me; for I wait on thee.

Psalm 25:21

Rest in the Lord, and wait patiently for him: fret not thyself because of him who prospereth in his way, because of the man who bringeth wicked devices to pass.

The steps of a good man are ordered by the Lord: and he delighteth in his way.

Though he fall, he shall not be utterly cast down: for the Lord upholdeth him with his hand.

Psalm 37:7,23,24

Wherefore seeing we also are compassed about with so great a cloud of witnesses, let us lay aside every weight, and the sin which doth so easily beset us, and let us run with patience the race that is set before us.

Hebrews 12:1

If any of you lack wisdom, let him ask of God, that giveth to all men liberally, and upbraideth not; and it shall be given him.

James 1:5

IF YOUR HUSBAND IS NOT A COMMITTED CHRISTIAN

Cast thy burden upon the Lord, and he shall sustain thee: he shall never suffer the righteous to be moved.

Psalm 55:22

And if it seem evil unto you to serve the Lord, choose you this day whom ye will serve.

Joshua 24:15a

And call upon me in the day of trouble: I will deliver thee, and thou shalt glorify me.

Psalm 50:15

He healeth the broken in heart, and bindeth up their wounds.

Psalm 147:3

Fear thou not; for I am with thee: be not dismayed; for I am thy God: I will strengthen thee; yea, I will help thee; yea, I will uphold thee with the right hand of my righteousness.

Behold, all they that were incensed against thee shall be ashamed and confounded: they shall be as nothing; and they that strive with thee shall perish.

Thou shalt seek them, and shalt not find them, even them that contended with thee: they that war against thee shall be as nothing, and as a thing of nought.

For I the Lord thy God will hold thy right hand, saying unto thee, Fear not; I will help thee.

Isaiah 41:10-13

For with God nothing shall be impossible.

Luke 1:37

For verily I say unto you, That whosoever shall say unto this mountain, Be thou removed, and be thou cast into the sea; and shall not doubt in his heart, but shall believe that those things which he saith shall come to pass; he shall have whatsoever he saith.

Mark 11:23

I came not to call the righteous, but sinners to repentance.

Luke 5:32

In your patience possess ye your souls.

Luke 21:19

For the Son of man is come to seek and to save that which was lost.

Luke 19:10

Thou therefore endure hardness, as a good soldier of Jesus Christ.

2 Timothy 2:3

IF YOUR HUSBAND IS NOT YOUR FAMILY'S SPIRITUAL LEADER

Shew me thy ways, O Lord; teach me thy paths.

What man is he that feareth the Lord? him shall he teach in the way that he shall choose.

Psalm 25:4,12

Now therefore go, and I will be with thy mouth, and teach thee what thou shalt say.

Exodus 4:12

Teach me thy way, O Lord, and lead me in a plain path, because of mine enemies.

Psalm 27:11

Teach me to do thy will; for thou art my God: thy spirit is good; lead me into the land of uprightness.

Psalm 143:10

Then Peter and the other apostles answered and said, We ought to obey God rather than men.

Acts 5:29

Keep my commandments, and live; and my law as the apple of thine eye.

Proverbs 7:2

If ye be willing and obedient, ye shall eat the good of the land:

But if ye refuse and rebel, ye shall be devoured with the sword: for the mouth of the Lord hath spoken it.

Isaiah 1:19,20

Wherefore gird up the loins of your mind, be sober, and hope to the end for the grace that is to be brought unto you at the revelation of Jesus Christ;

As obedient children, not fashioning yourselves according to the former lusts in your ignorance.

1 Peter 1:13,14

Servants, be obedient to them that are your masters according to the flesh, with fear and trembling, in singleness of your heart, as unto Christ;

With good will doing service, as to the Lord, and not to men.

Ephesians 6:5,7

Likewise, ye wives, be in subjection to your own husbands; that, if any obey not the word, they also may without the word be won by the conversation of the wives.

1 Peter 3:1

IF YOUR HUSBAND IS UNTALKATIVE OR DISTANT

That he would grant you, according to the riches of his glory, to be strengthened with might by his Spirit in the inner man.

Ephesians 3:16

But I will hope continually, and will yet praise thee more and more.

Psalm 71:14

For in thee, O Lord, do I hope: thou wilt hear, O Lord my God.

Psalm 38:15

Why art thou cast down, O my soul? and why art thou disquieted within me? hope in God: for I shall yet praise him, who is the health of my countenance, and my God.

Psalm 43:5

I am a companion of all them that fear thee, and of them that keep thy precepts.

Psalm 119:63

Happy is he that hath the God of Jacob for his help, whose hope is in the Lord his God.

Psalm 146:5

Blessed are the merciful: for they shall obtain mercy.

But I say unto you, That ye resist not evil: but whosoever shall smite thee on thy right cheek, turn to him the other also.

But I say unto you, Love your enemies, bless them that curse you, do good to them that hate you, and pray for them which despitefully use you, and persecute you.

Matthew 5:7,39,44

Hope deferred maketh the heart sick: but when the desire cometh, it is a tree of life.

Proverbs 13:12

And forgive us our debts, as we forgive our debtors.

For if ye forgive men their trespasses, your heavenly Father will also forgive you:

But if ye forgive not men their trespasses, neither will your Father forgive your trespasses.

Matthew 6:12,14,15

And God is able to make all grace abound toward you; that ye, always having all sufficiency in all things, may abound to every good work.

2 Corinthians 9:8

Now the God of hope fill you with all joy and peace in believing, that ye may abound in hope, through the power of the Holy Ghost.

Romans 15:13

Part III
What Others Say

God is a good God and His ways are perfect. We can eliminate much needless pain and misery from our lives just by following His ways.

Stormy Omartian

Lord, if someone pleases you, he or she pleases me.

Iverna Tompkins

God has a much higher opinion of me, and thinks much more highly of me than I do of myself.

Roberta Simpson

Even if you were the last person on earth, Jesus Christ still would have died for you.

Mary McLendon

I have found in my life and marriage that quarreling never pays — the truth is always lost.

Evelyn Miles

Prayer is not conquering God's reluctance but taking hold of God's willingness. (Phillip Brooks, author of "O Little Town of Bethlehem")

Elizabeth Sherrill

The task ahead of you is not as great as the power behind you.

Bunny Constantino

Worship is giving our love, thanks, and praise to God and proving these things by instant, joyful, whole obedience.

Joy Dawson

Don't wait for the Lord to change your circumstances; make yourself available for Him to change you.

> Dee Eastman

As a mother, my job is to take care of the possible and trust God with the impossible.

> Ruth Bell Graham

I have more faith in God's ability to speak to me, than in my own ability to hear Him.

> Jeanna Tomlinson

God doesn't use wastebaskets.

> Arvella Schuller

The word of God is a paradox. To weigh both sides, read it all — frequently — so that you can determine God's balance for you.

> Helene Barber

Worry is like a rocking chair: it gives you something to do, but doesn't get you anywhere.

> Marilyn Fitzgerald

Jesus' words are as jewels, treasures worth giving up all life's ambitions to find.

The Lord can do great things through those who don't care who gets the credit.

> Helen Pearson

The greatest gift that I can give my husband is to change.

> Mary Jane Wright

People and the world can fail you, but God is ever faithful and will never fail you.

Mrs. Lucas Halim

Don't expect praise but always deserve it.

Rexella Van Impe

Your children learn more of your faith during the bad times than they do during the good times.

Beverly LaHaye

Knowledge may make a man look big, but it is only love that can make him grow to his full stature.

Dorothy Jean Ligon

Every job is a self portrait of the person who does it. Autograph your work with excellence.

Charlene Jehle

My favorite question is the question God Himself asks over and over in Scriptures: "Is anything too hard for Me?" This always reminds me of how silly my doubts are. And I, with Sarah, Elizabeth, and others to whom God asked this, have to answer a resounding, "No, absolutely nothing is impossible with You, God!"

Marilyn Hogue

Proverbs 31 is one of my favorite passages. Verse 26 has been especially meaningful to me. *She openeth her mouth with wisdom; and in her tongue is the law of kindness.* My daily confession is: I have the wisdom of God and know how to act in every situation and circumstance I come up against today.

Peggy Capps

She opens her mouth with wisdom; and in her tongue is the law of kindness. (Proverbs 31:26).

We are living in days when mouths are open and tongues are busy! We must be sure that people hear wisdom and kindness from our lips.

You can be wise, but keep this wisdom to yourself. Wouldn't it be much better for you to share it with others and have your words bless needy souls around you?

Louise Sumrall

No problem is without a solution, no task too difficult, when I love Jesus and Jesus loves me.

Lily Goh

Did you ever see a worried sparrow?

Faeona Pratney

God has everything under control.

Gwen Wilkerson

Trifles make perfection, but perfection is no trifle.

Phyllis Schlafly

To spend little time with Jesus is to accomplish little in Jesus!

Carolyn Savelle

My favorite quote is one by Jim Elliott: "He is no fool who gives what he cannot keep to gain what he cannot lose."

Carolyn Mahaney

We need always keep in mind that our bodies are the temple of the Holy Spirit, and we are to honor and glorify Him in our bodies. Our physical health is largely a result of what we eat and drink — although our mental health also affects our physical health. We cannot be our best for God unless we are in the best of health.

Ruth Nell Deir

God never gives me a new task without the grace and tools to accomplish it to His glory.

Mary Jane Wright

When you don't forgive others, you burn the bridge over which you yourself must travel to receive God's forgiveness for yourself.

Dodie Osteen

Everything we do or say apart from love is a step in darkness.

Pat Harrison

What lies within us is far greater than what lies before us or lies behind us.

Virginia Otis

In counting the cost of conflict, we will do whatever it takes to be available and obedient to the Lord.

Leilani B. Watt

This one scripture, my "motto-scripture," has been a great blessing and foundation in my spiritual life: *And ye shall know the truth, and the truth shall make you free* (John 8:32).

Shirley Boone

If you can't sleep, don't count sheep — talk to the Shepherd!

JoAnn Sutton

What many will miss in activity, God will reveal in prayer.

Jesus is all there really is.

Anne Murchison

Faith is believing the incredible,
Seeing the invisible,
Achieving the impossible.

Betty Mills

When temptation knocks on your heart's door, ask Jesus to answer that door.

Babs Jarvis

At each time of my life, I can have the time of my life, if I'm giving the time of my life to Jesus.

Joyce Rogers

Don't dig up in doubt what you plant in faith.

Hava Katz

Often times Jesus uses difficult situations to refine and transform us even more into His likeness. So our prayer should be, "Change me, Lord," instead of, "Change my situation."

Dotty Duke

Discouragement is not of the Lord. When problems occur, it is our reminder to look to the Lord.

Nordis Christenson

PART IV
GETTING INTO THE WORD

31-Day

DEVOTIONAL

By

Dick Mills

DAY 1

In the beauties of holiness....
Psalm 110:3b

Before we accepted the Lord and became believers, sin had left us deformed and lacking in any spiritual beauty. When we invited Jesus into our hearts and lives, He came in bringing a total transformation.

We are now arrayed in a robe of His righteousness and an adornment which this verse calls **the beauties of holiness.** In the original Hebrew this word **beauties** is *hadar (haw-dawr')*. It is defined as "a glorious majesty, an ornament of splendor, magnificent decoration." In Isaiah 63:1 the root word from which *hadar* is derived is translated **glorious**. The Lord is said to be **glorious in his apparel**, or clothed with holy ornament.

If you are a Christian, you are wearing this apparel 24 hours a day. It goes with conversion and becomes the clothing of the redeemed.

In Hebrew **holiness** is *qodesh (ko'-desh)* and is defined as "ceremonially pure or morally clean."

It is the word used to pronounce a person or object purified, consecrated, dedicated, and set apart for sacred purposes. *Qodesh* is used of any person who devotes himself to the Lord.

Psalm 110:3 describes a group of volunteers who are free-will gifts in the military service of the Lord. Their distinctive feature is their holy adornment. For God's glory and to contrast His beauty with the ugliness of sin, these people are arrayed in beautiful holy garments. Each believer is dressed as one who performs a priestly function.

Did anyone ever tell you that you are beautiful? This verse says you are!

Day 2

**...Master, we have toiled all the night and
have taken nothing: nevertheless at thy word
I will let down the net.**

Luke 5:5

Here is a *rhema* promise for everyone who has
read the manual, followed all the rules and still
not attained the desired results. One leader
complained, ''I went to a church growth seminar.
While I was away some of the folks in the church
got discouraged and quit. When I got back home
from learning how to help the church grow, I had
fewer people than when I went away. I must be
doing something wrong.''

If anyone knew how to fish, it was Peter. Prior
to meeting Jesus, Peter had been a professional
fisherman. He knew about fish. He knew their
feeding habits, when and where to go looking for
them, and how to catch them.

Peter had fished right the evening before. He
knew that the fish fed at night up close to the
shore, so that's where he fished for them. Yet he
had caught nothing. Then along comes Jesus, a
carpenter, who tells him to do two things, both

contrary to all the rules of good fishing practice. First, He asks him to fish at the brightest time of the day. (Any lake fisherman knows that when the sun is on the water, the fish all go to the bottom of the lake.) Secondly, Jesus asks Peter to reverse his direction and fish out in the center of the lake rather than along the shore.

Peter knew the habits of fish. But he also knew the power of Jesus' Word. His response to these seemingly contradictory directions was, "Master, we have done it right, but have had no results. However, at Your *rhema* (Word), we will try it again Your way." The Lord's way worked! His way and His Word will work for us, too!

DAY 3

My soul followeth hard after thee....
Psalm 63:8

The Septuagint Greek Old Testament renders this verse: "My soul has been glued to you...." The verb in this sentence is a word which has to do with adhesive qualities. When we say we are going to "stick" with someone, we are very close to the meaning of "following hard" after the Lord.

The original Hebrew word translated **followeth hard** in this verse is *dabaq (daw-bak')*. It is defined as "to cling to, to adhere to firmly as if with glue." It also is used in a loving and devoted way to mean "to be attached to someone or something by the heart strings."

Dabaq also can be defined as "clinging to someone in affection or loyalty." It carries with it the idea of keeping very close to someone. This is what the psalmist is referring to when he says, "Lord, my soul follows hard after You." It is the same word as used in Genesis to describe what happens in marriage: A man shall leave his father and mother and shall "cleave" to his wife.

249

(Gen. 2:24.) In this verse the word **cleave** is *dabaq*. It expresses the concept of ''staying real close to someone.''

When you love, respect, and admire someone, you want to be as near that person as possible. The psalmist wanted to be close to the Lord. He told Him so. He was a worshipper who did not want to be at a distance from his God. He wanted to cling to Him like an adhesive. Because of his desire, David was increased greatly.

We can have the same spiritual desire with the same spiritual results. I think this is a good desire, don't you?

Day 4

**Cast thy burden upon the Lord, and he shall
sustain thee: he shall never suffer
the righteous to be moved.**

Psalm 55:22

This verse has a lot to say to us about personal challenge and encouragement. Its three main power words are: 1) **cast,** 2) **burden,** and 3) **sustain.**

Cast means "to throw, hurl, abandon, or toss away as no longer needed or wanted." It also means "to dispense with something in such a way as to have nothing more to do with it." Our cares and our burdens are to be thrown away, abandoned into God's care, dispensed with so that we have nothing more to do with them.

Burden is a word used to describe a load of anxiety that weighs a person down. It has to do with one's lot in life, his particular sphere of influence, his daily duties and responsibilities. Various Bible scholars have defined this expression **your burden** in the following ways: "God's gift to you," "your hope," "your cares," (LXX) "your allotment," "your portion" and "your cares,

251

travails, and troubles that go with your business or your occupation.''

Sustain is a good word. It has to do with upholding, feeding, nourishing, supporting, and taking care of. God gives us a life to live and then invites us to turn over to Him the weight of it all so He can carry us and the load.

Incidentally, Peter, quoting from the Septuagint Old Testament, gave us the same words in a New Testament setting: **casting all your care upon him; for he careth for you** (1 Pet. 5:7). God cares for you. Shift the load from you to Him. He knows what to do with it!

D<small>AY</small> 5

**For the wages of sin is death; but the gift of
God is eternal life through Christ Jesus our Lord.**

Romans 6:23

What a study in contrasts! Wages and gift.
These two words are so opposite in meaning that
we could easily overlook the full import of their
significance.

The Greek word translated **wages** is *opsonion*
(op-so'-nee-on). It is the word for subsistence or
salary. It involves the concept of a reward or
recompense for services rendered. Thus "the
wages of sin" refers to the payoff which comes
as a result of serving Satan. The deceptive thing
about sin is that it so often comes disguised as
pleasure and fulfillment. Here, Paul is saying that
the devil is a deceiver who lures people into a life
of sin by promising them all kinds of future bliss.
However, the real payoff for all their hard work
(yes, sinners work real hard at sinning!) is
disintegration, destruction, and death.

The *gift* of God. What a beautiful contrast to
the wages of sin. The original Greek word for **gift**

is *charisma (khar'-is-mah)*, meaning "an endowment, something given freely." God freely bestows grace (unmerited favor) on those who call upon His name. Blessings, benefits, and bestowments all come to us from a loving, heavenly Father Who gives, and gives, and keeps on giving — because it is His nature to give.

The wages of death is earned. The gift of life is freely received. Before conversion we were on Satan's payroll, now we are on God's gift list! Satan's final payoff is death, but God's ultimate gift is eternal life. Which do you prefer: death or life? wages or gifts?

DAY 6

**But without faith it is impossible
to please him. . . .**

Hebrews 11:6a

What is faith? It is a combination of several
things:

TRUST: Faith enables us to approach the Lord
in trust. It causes us to say by our actions: "Lord,
I trust You. Your Word says You can be trusted
and I believe it." Faith in God is trust in God.

CONFIDENCE: Faith enables us to approach
the Lord with confidence. Our confidence is not
in the abilities, cleverness or ingenuity of man —
but of God. Faith is confidence that God will keep
His promises.

ASSURANCE: Assurance tells us that God
is everything His Word says He is. It tells us
that He is intervening on our behalf and for our
deliverance. Faith is assurance.

COURAGE: Faith is the courage needed to
approach God with a long list of needs and know
He hears our prayers and answers them for His
glory and honor. It is the courage to look to the

255

Lord in any time of need and not allow our circumstances to intimidate us or dictate to us.

ACTION: Faith has a passive side. It can be received as a gift from God. It also has an active side. Faith prompts action. Hebrews 11:33 tells us that faith *subdued*, faith *worked*, faith *obtained*, and faith even *stopped the mouth of lions*.

One scholar has stated: ''Faith's inner conviction about God is always translated into action and results in a lifestyle through which the reality of faith is expressed.''

DAY 7

Thou wilt keep him in perfect peace, whose mind is stayed on thee: because he trusteth in thee.

Isaiah 26:3

Part One

Perfect peace is a good translation of this phrase from the Hebrew Old Testament. In the original text the words read *shalom shalom*. This double word indicates a dual peace internally and externally.

This verse promises us an inner peace that stays with us 24 hours a day. According to Romans 14:17 the kingdom of God within us is righteousness, peace and joy in the Holy Ghost. Isaiah 32:17 promises us a work of inner peace that will also bring us calm confidence, settled assurance, and abiding trust. This inner peace is the one quality that can hold us together when everything in the world about us is falling apart. When you read the newspaper and find Bible prophecies being fulfilled, you may wonder how God's people are going to survive all the violence and turmoil ahead. Inner peace is the sustainer which will assure our holding steady in a turbulent world.

This verse also promises an external peace. Inner-city Christians have discovered this peace. Soldiers on the battlefield and workers in hectic offices and noisy factories have learned to draw from it. Once, where I worked there was a fellow employee who enjoyed heckling me. I called on God in prayer and He gave me this verse: **When a man's ways please the Lord, He maketh even his enemies to be at peace with him** (Prov. 16:7). As a result, an external peace came into a work place where turmoil and confusion had reigned before. I discovered and enjoyed both inner and outer peace in that situation.

DAY 8

Thou wilt keep him in perfect peace, whose mind is stayed on thee: because he trusteth in thee.

Isaiah 26:3

Part Two

A mind *stayed* on the Lord. Have you ever wondered what that means? In the original Hebrew text the word translated **stayed** is *camak* (*saw-mak'*) which is defined in its reflexive form as "to lean upon." One older grammarian consulted described the action expressed by *camak* as "to place or lay something upon an object so that it rests upon and is totally supported by that object." The word thus contains the idea of something's being undergirded, upheld or sustained so that it remains firm and unmoved.

When a person's mind is "leaning on" the Lord, the peace promised him is sure and perpetual. You and I can lean on the Almighty continually and His peace will be ours continually. This "leaning" is an attitude of mind which gives God the benefit of every doubt and question; it trusts Him unequivocally and believes implicitly that all things work together for good to those who love Him.

When the Bible says that David was a man after God's own heart, it is speaking of direction. It is saying that David's inclinations (his leanings) were toward the Lord. David sought after God. He even pursued Him. David was always headed in God's direction. We can display this same kind of continual pursuit of the Lord by having a heart which is always hungry for Him.

One way to transform Isaiah 26:3 into a personal confession is to state: ''The Lord will watch over me and guard me with an internal and an external peace because my mind and its thoughts are ever leaning in His direction.''

DAY 9

...Freely ye have received, freely give.
Matthew 10:8

I once knew of a father whose children craved attention from him. He seemingly was not able to give them the love they wanted from him. He went to the Lord in prayer and asked why he could not give the affection his offspring desired.

The Lord relayed this thought to his mind: "How can you give something to someone else that you have never received yourself?" The man realized that since he had never received parental affection himself, he had none to offer his own children.

The Lord did bless this father with an understanding of His love for us. Through Romans 5:5, the Lord showed him that unselfish, caring, giving, *agape* love is poured into our hearts by the Father, resides in us by the Son, and flows out of us by the Holy Spirit.

In life there are many things that we do not have. Consequently, we cannot give them to others. But there are many things we do have and can give. What you have freely received, that freely give.

We have received forgiveness. We are capable of forgiving.

We have received peace. We can give peace.

We have received light. We have light to share with others.

We have received joy. Let's pass it on.

At our conversion God poured His *agape* love into us. We have that love to give. As the Armed Forces advertisement says: "It's a great place to start!"

DAY 10

**...My presence shall go with thee,
and I will give thee rest.**

Exodus 33:14

Rest is total absence from stress, conflict, turmoil, tension and hassle. This is not a rest "from" activity, but a rest "in" the midst of activity. Have you not been impressed by certain people who seem to be the epitome of composure and total serenity while everyone else around them is going to pieces or "coming unglued"? What is it that allows these people to show such inner strength and continual tranquility?

Years ago, the old saints of God called this state of continual peace and quiet "the rest of faith." The writer of Hebrews assures us: **There remaineth therefore a rest for the people of God** (Heb. 4:9). He also exhorts us to make every effort to enter into that rest. This rest is a place of faith that allows us to function free of stress, tension, and pressure. In that place we can be at rest while going about our normal activities of life, while busy with our responsibilities. This almost seems like a contradiction in terms: resting while

263

laboring...resting while exerting energy. This is not laziness, shirking duties, neglecting responsibilities, or sleeping on guard.

Rest is the capacity to function at full capacity and strength all the while sustained by an "in-working," "in-strengthening," God-given ability. Jesus as our role model is a good example. He was never caught off guard or taken by surprise. Even when trick questions were thrown at Him, He handled His opponents with a disarming ease. His inner peace kept Him unruffled even in the face of resistance and opposition. In this verse, He promises us that same inner peace and rest.

Day 11

And when they began to sing and to praise, the Lord set ambushments against the children of Ammon, Moab, and mount Seir, which were come against Judah; and they were smitten.

2 Chronicles 20:22

Think of it! Singing and praising your way to victory. Singing and praising your way through discouragement, oppression, depression, fear, and worry.

. . . and they were three days in gathering of the spoil (the loot), **it was so much** (v. 25). In Bible days, driving an enemy out entitled the victor to all the spoils of battle. The army of Judah so routed the enemy that it took them three days to collect all the booty the enemy had left behind. And the victory was wrought not by fighting but by singing and praising the Lord!

God responded to the prayers of His people with these reassuring words: **. . . the battle is not yours, but God's** (v. 15). With this assurance, the king of Judah appointed singers and praisers to go out before the army and to praise the Lord. When they began to sing and praise, the enemy

265

was defeated. The key word in this passage is **began**. Your victory is dependent upon your doing something. You need to *begin*. To begin to count your blessings. To begin to enumerate past deliverances. To begin to praise the Lord. To begin to sing your song of deliverance.

The Bible says that the Lord inhabits the praises of His people. (Ps. 22:3.) When the Lord's presence comes into our setting of praise and worship, the enemy is powerless against us. We can literally sing our way through every battle and win the victory the same way Jehoshaphat's army won. Singing and praising the Lord is an effective weapon in our spiritual warfare!

D~AY~ 12

**But without faith it is impossible
to please him....**

Hebrews 11:6

According to scripture, pleasing the Lord is
within the reach of all of us. Out of the Dark Ages
came a concept of God as One Who was vindic-
tive. He angrily watched every move people
made. If they strayed or erred one bit, He was
quick to "zap" them. He was out to get people.
Unfortunately, this concept still exists today.
Sadly, it disregards everything the Word of God
has to say about His goodness and merciful
lovingkindness.

Our heavenly Father says in His Word that
there are things we can do to please Him. They
are not impossible. Having faith and trust in Him
pleases Him. Colossians 3:20 tells us that God is
pleased when children obey their parents. Second
Samuel 7:29 indicates that it pleases God to bless
our homes. Keeping His commandments is pleasing in His sight. (1 John 3:22.) Any recognition
or acknowledgement we give to His righteous
Word is well-pleasing to the Lord, according to

Isaiah 42:21. The psalmist tells us that praising, singing, and worshipping the Lord pleases Him. (Ps. 69:30,31.) Solomon says that our journey or pathway can be pleasing to God, resulting in His favor and blessing. (Prov. 16:7.) In Isaiah 55:11, the Lord Himself tells us that His Word will not return to Him void (unfulfilled or unrealized) but will accomplish what He pleases, and will prosper in the thing for which He sent it. The writer of Hebrews says that Enoch had . . . **this testimony, that he pleased God** (Heb. 11:5.) If you look up the words *please* and *pleased* in the concordance, you will be happily surprised to discover how often things were said and done that pleased the Lord.

Day 13

**I will instruct thee and teach thee in
the way which thou shalt go; I will
guide thee with mine eye.**

Psalm 32:8

This is a good verse for those of us who seek
guidance and direction from the Lord. It is an
assurance that our heavenly Father is going to
move us from a weak transmission to a "clear-
channel station with no static" so we will be able
to hear the gentle voice of the Good Shepherd
without interference.

The Lord makes three direct promises in this
verse:

1) **I will instruct thee....** This is like having a
private tutor. The purpose of the instruction we
thus receive is to make us more intelligent, skillful
and circumspect in our dealings, more adept in
making decisions.

2) **...and teach thee in the way which thou shalt
go;...** The original word used here indicates the
pointing of a finger in a certain direction. It also
implies shooting an arrow at a target in such a

269

way as to avoid missing the mark. This word from the Lord is an assurance that we will not drift aimlessly through life, but that He will give us a definite direction and a clear goal to aim for.

3) ...**I will guide thee with mine eye.** One translation of this phrase says: "I will keep my eye upon you to see how you are doing."

Here is my paraphrase of this verse: "I will make you skillful and proficient in decision-making and will aim you in the right direction; I will watch your progress and see how you are getting along; My eye will be upon you for your benefit."

D<small>AY</small> 14

...He hath made us accepted in the beloved.

Ephesians 1:6

Accepted in the Beloved. What an encouraging word. In this world, with its constant search for affection, approval, and acceptance, it is good to know that we Christians are accepted in the Beloved. We do not have to struggle for acceptance, we already have it. How comforting to know that our Father will not love us any more (or less!) in the future than He does right now.

Sometimes the best way to understand a word is to find out how it is used elsewhere. This word *accepted* is no exception. In the original Greek text, it is *charitoo (khar-ee-to'-o)*, and is closely related to the grace word *charis. Charitoo* is defined as "highly favored," "graced with honor," and "accepted." It only appears one other time in the New Testament and that is in Luke 1:28 when the angel appeared to Mary and called her by this name: **Hail, thou that art highly favored, the Lord is with thee: blessed art thou among women.** The word used to tell Mary that she was highly favored by being selected by the Lord for a very special task is the same word used to describe all Christians. We have also been highly favored by being selected of God.

Mary was chosen to bring about the Lord's first coming into the world. All believers have been chosen to bring about the Lord's Second Coming into the world.

Quit putting yourself down. If you are a Christian, you are not an outcast, you are *charitoo* — accepted in the Beloved!

D<small>AY</small> 15

...Some say...Elias, and others Jeremias....
Matthew 16:14

Jesus had just asked His disciples how the world viewed Him. They relayed to their Master that people saw Him in different capacities. Some felt He was a reflection of Elijah, while others felt He was of the Jeremiah mold. The thing that is interesting here is that Jesus is a fine blend of many characteristics of both men which we would do well to emulate.

Elijah was Mr. Firm. He was as straight as an arrow. One of his many positive qualities was manliness. He was strong spiritually, physically, mentally, emotionally, and volitionally. Elijah comes across as a no-nonsense type with unusual strength of character, intense spiritual drive, and a determined will. The people saw these same qualities in Jesus when He refused to be intimidated by the religious leaders. It was easy to associate Jesus with Elijah because of His strength.

273

Jeremiah was the exact opposite. He was gentle, compassionate, kind, merciful, patient, genteel. He was known to weep openly, was highly sensitive, and had a great capacity for love and kindness. Like Jeremiah, Jesus was tenderhearted and possessed great feelings.

Put Elijah and Jeremiah together and you have a person who is tough but gentle, firm but compassionate, rugged and strong but blessed with great sensitivity. It would be good if each of us could incorporate these same qualities in our own life. We too need to be firm against sin, but compassionate with the sinner. What an ideal!

Day 16

**...thine enemies shall be found liars unto
thee; and thou shalt tread upon their high places.**

Deuteronomy 33:29

He was in tears and visibly shaken by his
circumstances. He was the proprietor of a local
doughnut shop and had been doing well until
trouble came his way. An unscrupulous person
came into his store and staged a phony accidental
fall. Right behind the "injured party" was a
person with a camera to take a picture of the
"accident." Behind that person was another man
ready to take down the names of convenient
"witnesses." A lawsuit for an exorbitant sum of
money was then filed by the "victim" who had
staged the whole scenario.

This dear brother told me, "Dick, I could lose
it all. My insurance policy for this type of accident
is minimal at best. If this fellow wins this case,
I could lose everything I own." I stood in agreement with the shopkeeper, praying with him that
the Lord would work a miracle of deliverance.
How I appreciate the faithfulness of the Lord
in these situations. I was not familiar with

Deuteronomy 33:29, but the Holy Spirit quickened it to me: "All your enemies shall be found as liars unto you."

The next day, in his private chambers, the judge in charge of the case began to read over the records. The trial was to start in one hour. Suddenly the magistrate was heard to make this statement in disgust: "This is a travesty of justice. The plaintiff is obviously a pathological liar. I refuse to hear this case. I am throwing it out of court."

An overnight fulfillment of a word from the Lord! Case dismissed! Another enemy found as a liar!

DAY 17

**...Greater is he that is in you,
than he that is in the world.**

1 John 4:4

Someone once asked me why a football never gets deflated in a game. Twenty-two huge, burly men kick it, throw it, pounce on it, fumble it — yet it never gets "squashed" or loses its size to deflation. The answer is a simple law of physics. It seems that the internal pressure of the ball is much greater than all the pressure 22 men can place upon it externally.

This verse says the same thing about us as Christians. The power of the Holy Spirit residing in our hearts and lives is greater than all the pressure the external world can place upon us.

You could list all the different opponents who come against you to impede or block your forward progress. Satan's strategy is to deflate you and render you inoperative, but the Holy Ghost gives you a buoyancy. You can roll with the punches. It may seem sometimes that you are being tossed around by circumstances, but with the Lord's power within, you will always bounce back.

This verse is a great comfort to many people who are not having it very easy in life. It is a constant reminder of God's sustaining grace, Christ's resident peace, and the Holy Spirit's indwelling power. Greater is the power within us than the pressure upon us. So hang in there, teammate; despite the hard knocks, we're winning!

DAY 18

**If the iron be blunt, and he do not whet the edge,
then must he put to more strength.**

Ecclesiastes 10:10

Sometimes we have to make serious decisions
that mean severing someone or something from
our life. We painfully face the prospect of making
unpleasant "cuts." A long-time employee must
be released. A major household move has to
be undertaken. (Sometimes moving from one
location to another is as disruptive to a family as
chopping is to a tree.) A life-time behavior pattern
has to be changed drastically. All these "cuts" are
hard, but they don't have to be brutal or bloody.

This verse tells us that a sharp cutting edge
makes the difference. Dullness means that our
action done in the power of the flesh will not only
require much more strength, but will also be
messier.

Jesus prayed all night before making His
greatest decisions or changes. You and I rush in
with a dull axe and chop away, but it is preferable
to face major "cuts" with spiritual preparation.

Fasting and prayer will sharpen the cutting edge of our faithful action.

Sometimes removal of persons from our association is like a surgeon cutting away an abscessed part of the body. With skill and speed he makes a deft incision, removes the poisonous mass, closes up the wound, and lets the healing process begin. The sharper the cutting edge, the quicker the recovery.

This verse urges "sharpness" in removing unpleasant elements that are keeping our "tree of life" from becoming as healthy and vigorous as it should be. Prayer "sharpens" us up for even the distasteful things we are called to do.

DAY 19

...a merry heart hath a continual feast.

Proverbs 15:15

A feast is more than an ordinary meal. It includes the idea of company, music, entertainment, unusual or special gourmet foods. In general, a feast involves eating plus having a good time.

In our world, we see a great pursuit of "good times." People are trying so hard to find pleasure and satisfaction. You often hear the question, "Are we having fun yet?" The world is trying to find the right things in all the wrong places.

In John 4:32, the Lord Jesus told His disciples, **...I have meat to eat that ye know not of.** Our text verse confirms this truth. *The Amplified Bible* version reads: **...he who has a glad heart has a continual feast [regardless of circumstances].**

Believers do not have to spend a lot of money to go to a music concert. They have a song going on inside of them continuously. It is the song of the Lord. Jesus is singing it within their hearts. (Zeph. 3:17.) Christians don't have to wait up to

281

hear some stand-up comedian on T.V. tell the latest jokes. They have the joy of the Lord within them giving them "a merry heart."

When the world comes up with a booklet called "How to Party Every Night of the Week," the Christian's response is, "I don't have to clutter my life with a lot of socializing; I'm so contented serving the Lord that I don't need partying."

The joy of the Lord is like a continuous feast. We are not anti-social, just contented and happy. We don't have to go around looking for what we have already found.

DAY 20

**He shall not be afraid of evil tidings:
his heart is fixed, trusting in the Lord.**

Psalm 112:7

Out of our twentieth-century culture there has come a familiar expression, ''getting a fix.'' This term usually refers to taking drugs. Because of his dependency upon artificial stimulants, the drug addict is continually in the position of craving a ''fix.''

In this verse, David states that the person who trusts in God is never really afraid because his heart is ''fixed'' on the Lord. That's good news for us today, because in our society it seems that everyone has a dependency of some kind.

Materialistic people are dependent upon money for their happiness. Egocentric performing artists must have a continual supply of adulation and applause from their adoring fans. Authority figures are driven by a consuming hunger for power. Perverts have an insatiable appetite for ''kinky'' sex. Alcoholics lust after liquor to slake their never-ending thirst. Smokers crave nicotine constantly. Drug addicts are enslaved by their continual need of a "fix."

We Christians are dependent also. The difference is, we look to the Lord as our sole source of supply. Our dependence is on Him. This is not a mark of weakness; it is a mark of intelligence. Our reliance is upon the only absolutely dependable thing in the universe: the Lord Jesus Christ. Our heart is "fixed," because we trust in Him.

DAY 21

Go ye therefore and teach all nations....
Matthew 28:19

This verse begins with the familiar injunction, **Go ye**.... This has probably been the one phrase which, more than any other, has inspired believers in every age to go forth to mission fields and proclaim sacrificially the Good News. "Go ye" has a certain ring to it. It is a commanding imperative. It motivates believers for a commitment to a life of unselfishness. "Go ye" moves people to disregard creature comforts and to boldly declare with the hymnist: "I'll go where you want me to go, dear Lord, O'er mountain or plain or sea; — I'll say what you want me to say, dear Lord, I'll be what you want me to be."

In addition to the challenging command "go ye," there is another option, an alternative reading of this verse. Besides "go ye," the opening phrase can be interpreted, "As you go...."

All Christians are in motion. We are on a path leading to our eternal home. We are going through this life, led by the Spirit, and strengthened by the Word of God.

"As you go, make disciples of all nations." When you go to the post office, when you go to the store, when you go to work, to school, or to church. When you go on vacation. Whenever and wherever you go, be on the lookout for opportunities to share with others the Good News!

Not only go, but as you go — make disciples!

Day 22

**This is the day which the Lord hath made;
we will rejoice and be glad in it.**

Psalm 118:24

Which day is this verse talking about? Is it confined to one isolated day in human history?

The "day which the Lord hath made" began with the day of creation when morning stars sang together and all the sons of God shouted for joy. (Job 38:7.)

Another day of rejoicing occurred when Israel was led out of bondage in Egypt. David spoke of this day, saying of the Lord: **. . . he brought forth his people with joy, and his chosen with gladness** (Ps. 105:43).

That was a day of joyful deliverance. But it was not the only one. The day of Jesus' resurrection from the dead is also included in this verse. The anguish of the disciples, the sorrow of the women, the heavy gloom of the crucifixion — all this was replaced by the joy of an empty tomb: **. . . Then were the disciples glad, when they saw the** (risen) **Lord** (John 20:20).

287

Other days of rejoicing are the day of our own personal conversion, the day set aside each week to worship in the house of the Lord, and the day the Lord returns to claim His Bride, the Church.

Besides all these special days, let us remember that this age is often referred to as ''the Gospel day.'' It is a day of God's making and its blessings are ours because our Lord has been placed as the head of the corner.

So therefore every day we live is the Lord's day and is a cause of joyous celebration!

DAY 23

**Let your speech be alway with grace,
seasoned with salt, that ye may know
how ye ought to answer each man.**

Colossians 4:6

There is a vast difference between salty speech and speech seasoned with salt. Salty speech is offensive, sarcastic, sharp, bitter, biting. Speech seasoned with salt is attractive, appetizing, flavorful, tasteful. It fulfills the very words of Jesus who urged His disciples to "have salt in yourselves." (Mark 9:50).

In sharing our faith with others, we need to be able to capture their interest and keep their attention. One way to do that is to make sure that our speech is well seasoned with salt. Just as salt adds appeal to food, so it adds appeal to our witness to others.

Salt enhances and enriches; it adds flavor to that which is dull, bland, and tasteless. Well seasoned speech adds flavor to the Bread of Life which we share with others to enhance and enrich their lives.

Salt is used as a preservative; it prevents corruption in meat. Likewise, "the meat of the Word" which we share with others can be kept pure and incorrupt when our speech is well seasoned with salt.

Salt produces thirst. Well salted speech can actually stimulate a thirst for the Water of Life.

In his New Testament commentary, Dean Alford states: "Salt as used by our Savior symbolizes the unction, freshness and vital briskness which characterizes the Holy's Spirit's presence and work in a man."

Without salt in our speech, our words will be insipid, banal, and uninspiring. Prayer makes the difference. A consistent life of daily prayer keeps the salt in our lives from losing its savor.

DAY 24

**But God forbid that I should glory, save in the
cross of our Lord Jesus Christ, by whom the world
is crucified unto me, and I unto the world.**

Galatians 6:14

After having preached a milestone message in
a Southern California town, I was interviewed by
a reporter from a local newspaper who wrote an
article claiming that I had preached 2,500 times
in ten years. That unsolicited notoriety made me
wonder: Would Paul have wanted his ministry
glorified that way? Surely not.

Some ministries publish how many countries
they are reaching, how many churches they have
established, how many missionaries they are
supporting, how many busses they run each
Sunday, how many people their sanctuary holds,
how many different choirs they maintain, how
many converts they have won, and on and on.

I once knew of a ministry whose leaders
boasted that they had the largest staff of any
church in the country. After getting into financial
difficulty, they called in a management consultant
team who advised them that they were greatly

291

overstaffed. To stay afloat, they were forced to let 200 church workers go. Very soon afterwards, those same leaders were once again boasting: this time that they had one of the smallest staffs in one of America's largest churches!

In an age that is impressed with success, with bigness and with numbers, this verse reminds us of where our priorities really are. Part of the crucifixion to the world of which Paul is speaking here is a death to the "numbers game." It includes pride of grace, pride of race, pride of face, and pride of place.

Do you think we Christians will ever learn that God is not impressed with *our* achievements?

DAY 25

**...The beloved of the Lord shall
dwell in safety by him....**

Deuteronomy 33:12

In a world full of evil, violence, and hatred, it is comforting to be promised *safety*. This word is vast and all-inclusive. Besides personal protection, it includes confidence, trust, security, and freedom from danger or fear. The original Hebrew word translated **safety** here is *betach (beh'-takh)*, meaning "a place of refuge." Thus this verse confidently assures us of our welfare and survival despite the vigors and uncertainties of this present unsettled age.

The beloved of the Lord includes all believers in Jesus Christ, especially those who are serving Him and doing His will. In Ephesians 1:6, the Apostle Paul declares that we believers are **...accepted in the beloved.** Acceptance by the Lord does not mean haughty exclusivism, privileged elitism, or entrance into a special inner circle. It simply makes possible that close personal relationship which exists between God and *all* those who will freely receive His gracious love.

293

The Bride of Christ is composed of redeemed people who are in many different stages of spiritual development. Regardless of our current level of spirituality, all of us make up the Beloved. As such, we are all promised safety, security, and confidence. We may think the Lord has "pets," "favorites," and "choice saints," those who have "an inside track" to His blessings or who enjoy a special "hot line" connection with Heaven. That is not so. We are all equal recipients of God's saving grace and therefore equal beneficiaries of His promised watchcare and safekeeping.

DAY 26

And I will rebuke the devourer for your sakes....
Malachi 3:11

The **devourer** needs to be defined. The Hebrew word *akal (aw-kal')* means "to eat, consume or burn up." It was used by Bible writers to define the actions of drought, famine, war, pestilence, and plague. To "rebuke the devourer" is to check, curb, and deter anything that consumes time, energy, or cash-flow.

In this verse the Lord promises to put a stopgap on that which consumes our time. How many times have you started out a day with a plan for getting things done, only to look back at the end of the day and realize that your time had gotten away from you? The Lord has promised to rebuke the devourer of time.

The same promise applies to energy. During the average eight-hour workday, we expect to achieve a stated number of goals, to complete so many assigned tasks, to produce a certain predetermined amount of output for our efforts. It is always disconcerting to look back at the end of the day and compare how much we intended to get done with how little we actually accomplished. The Lord has promised to rebuke the devourer of energy.

This promise also applies to money. You buy tires, and they wear out too soon. You buy shoes, and they do not last. You buy groceries, and run out before the week is over. You spend money, yet have nothing to show for it. God has promised to rebuke the devourer of finances.

With God's blessings, you and I can get 60 minutes of time out of every hour, eight hours of productivity out of each working day, and a hundred pennies of value out of every dollar spent. What a blessing!

DAY 27

**I sent you to reap that whereon ye bestowed
no labour: other men laboured, and ye are
entered into their labours.**

John 4:38

There are sowers and there are reapers.
Preliminary work and preparation is often done
by those who never get to see the result of their
labors. Those who do the planting have to believe
that their contribution is going to terminate in a
good harvest, whether they get to experience the
joy of gathering that harvest or not.

Here, however, the emphasis is reversed. The
Lord Jesus tells His disciples that they are going
to reap a harvest planted by someone who
preceded them. He could be referring to Old
Testament workers, to John the forerunner, or to
Himself.

Our Lord is saying to His disciples: ''I am
sending you in to reap a harvest. Others ahead
of you have done all the preliminary preparation.
The ground work has been taken care of. All you
have to do is reap the benefits of their labor.''

297

Prophetically speaking, this verse could apply to you and me. Nearly two thousand years of planting, sowing, irrigating, weeding, hoeing, and cultivating have gone into the Gospel ministry. It is now harvesttime, time to reap all the benefits and blessings that go with the worldwide harvest of souls for the kingdom. The early evangelists, intercessors, and soulwinners have done their part. Now it's our turn. Our part is to enter their labors and gather in the harvest they have made possible. The fields are white unto harvest. The time is now!

DAY 28

**...the love of God is shed abroad in our hearts
by the Holy Ghost which is given unto us.**

Romans 5:5

Here is a promise of an abundance of *agape*
love, the God-like love which gives expecting
nothing in return. This promise has to do with
loving the unlovely, those who cannot, or will not,
return that love. This verse means a great deal to
missionaries who give up creature comforts and
personal ease among their own people in order
to take the Gospel message to a foreign people
far away who many times neither desire nor
appreciate such personal sacrifice on their behalf.

"Yankee, go home!" is not just a political
slogan. Often it is the "buzz word" American
missionaries of all denominations and churches
hear from hostile nationals who misunderstand
and resent their "intrusion" into their everyday
lives.

What would prompt a person to leave familiar
and pleasant surroundings and go hundreds,
even thousands, of miles away to invest his life

in a strange, uncomfortable and often dangerous environment? Especially when that sacrifice seems to be neither recognized nor rewarded? Those missionaries I talk to share how the *agape* love of God so overwhelmed them that they had no other choice but to respond to the call to the mission field. That love so motivated them that they would only complain if they did *not* get to go.

God's love is the greatest power in the universe. Once people see and recognize the reality of that love demonstrated before them, their response changes from "Yankee, go home!" to "Friend, please stay and tell us more about this Jesus!" That makes it all worthwhile!

Day 29

**Thou shalt increase my greatness,
and comfort me on every side.**

Psalm 71:21

In the original Hebrew version, the word translated **comfort** is *nacham (naw-kham')*. It describes God's response to our trying circumstances.

One definition of *nacham* is "to sigh." The prophet Isaiah says of God and His people: **In all their affliction, he was afflicted....** (Is. 63:9). The writer of Hebrews tells us that we have a High Priest Who is touched with the feelings of our infirmities. (Heb. 4:15.) So when circumstances cause us to sigh, the Lord sighs with us. But, He does infinitely more than that.

Another definition of *nacham* is "to breathe strongly" or "to draw breath forcibly." We do this in times of strong physical or emotional stress. We breathe hard when excited, when forced to move rapidly, or when the pace of our lives is drastically speeded up. When the Lord says through the psalmist that He will comfort us, He is saying that

301

He will be right by our side. Our eagerness, excitement and enthusiasm become His eagerness, excitement, enthusiasm. In stressing that the spirit (Spirit) is *willing*, the Bible uses a word that describes ardent eagerness. Our God is just as eager for our victory as we are.

Another definition of *nacham* is "to pity," implying feeling such sorrow for a person as to step in and avenge him against his adversary. Gesenius, the grammarian, says of *nacham:* "It includes the notion of God putting forth help and taking vengeance."

Our God does much more than console us in our battles; He takes our side with us against our enemy!

DAY 30

**. . . let us offer the sacrifice of praise to God
continually, that is, the fruit of our lips, giving
thanks to his name.**

Hebrews 13:15

A sacrifice is something of value which is freely
given up by one person in order to please,
enhance, or benefit another. Jesus' death on the
cross is an example of the supreme sacrifice. He
freely offered up His life for us human beings in
order to accomplish for us what we could never
do for ourselves, pay the full price of our
redemption from our sins.

The sacrifice of praise is something we offer
up to our Lord. A sacrifice requires self-denial.
Just as Jesus voluntarily gave up His life for our
sakes, though He despised the cross, so we give
Him the praise and thanksgiving due Him,
though we may not always feel like doing so.

If ours is to be a true sacrifice, we cannot wait
for favorable circumstances before we offer it. We
are to offer up praise and thanks continually. Such
praise is not always a sincere expression of the
heart. Sometimes the fruit of our lips can be the

303

most shallow effort imaginable. Phonetically, all the lips can do is enunciate sounds. Those sounds alone do not necessarily constitute true praise. It is when the lips overflow with that which is welling up in our innermost being that we produce the real fruit of praise.

However, even if our praise does seem superficial and shallow, it is still highly acceptable as a sacrifice to the Lord. God does not require us to feel, only to acknowledge: **Let every thing that hath breath praise the Lord** (Ps. 150:6).

Day 31

**...Judah shall again take root
downward, and bear fruit upward.**

Isaiah 37:31

A tree grows in three directions: downward,
upward, and outward. This verse promises
growth and expansion in two of the three
directions, both down and up at the same time.
The message is that our growth as Christians is
recognizable by ourselves, by the Lord's angelic
host, and by others as well.

Taking root downward is progess known only
to us. The root system is below the surface and
not visible to anyone. In the course of a year, there
is growth, but it is undetected. You and I are not
the same people we were a year ago. Perhaps
others cannot see the deepening process at work,
but we know it is there.

Bearing fruit upward has visible results. Fruit
bearing is an activity that is open and apparent
to any observer. Fruit is the end result of a year's
special effort. It is for all to see and enjoy.

305

Bearing fruit is also another word for productivity. When Jesus said that we would be able to judge a tree by its fruit, He was telling us to be observant of our own lives, as well as others', because we show what we are by what we produce.

The ring on the inside of a tree may be minuscule and totally hidden from human view. But year in and year out, it records a message: this tree is growing and producing fruit. Visible and invisible growth is taking place.

You and I should be encouraged! The Lord has promised us continuous and on-going growth!

READING THE BIBLE
IN ONE YEAR

January

1 Gen. 1-2; Ps. 1; Matt. 1-2
2 Gen. 3-4; Ps. 2; Matt. 3-4
3 Gen. 5-7; Ps. 3; Matt. 5
4 Gen. 8-9; Ps. 4; Matt. 6-7
5 Gen. 10-11; Ps. 5; Matt. 8-9
6 Gen. 12-13; Ps. 6; Matt. 10-11
7 Gen. 14-15; Ps. 7; Matt. 12
8 Gen. 16-17; Ps. 8; Matt. 13
9 Gen. 18-19; Ps. 9; Matt. 14-15
10 Gen. 20-21; Ps. 10; Matt. 16-17
11 Gen. 22-23; Ps. 11; Matt. 18
12 Gen. 24; Ps. 12; Matt. 19-20
13 Gen. 25-26; Ps. 13; Matt. 21
14 Gen. 27-28; Ps. 14; Matt. 22
15 Gen. 29-30; Ps. 15; Matt. 23
16 Gen. 31-32; Ps. 16; Matt. 24
17 Gen. 33-34; Ps. 17; Matt. 25
18 Gen. 35-36; Ps. 18; Matt. 26
19 Gen. 37-38; Ps. 19; Matt. 27
20 Gen. 39-40; Ps. 20; Matt. 28
21 Gen. 41-42; Ps. 21; Mark 1
22 Gen. 43-44; Ps. 22; Mark 2
23 Gen. 45-46; Ps. 23; Mark 3
24 Gen. 47-48; Ps. 24; Mark 4
25 Gen. 49-50; Ps. 25; Mark 5
26 Ex. 1-2; Ps. 26; Mark 6
27 Ex. 3-4; Ps. 27; Mark 7
28 Ex. 5-6; Ps. 28; Mark 8
29 Ex. 7-8; Ps. 29; Mark 9
30 Ex. 9-10; Ps. 30; Mark 10
31 Ex. 11-12; Ps. 31; Mark 11

February

1   Ex. 13-14; Ps. 32; Mark 12
2   Ex. 15-16; Ps. 33; Mark 13
3   Ex. 17-18; Ps. 34; Mark 14
4   Ex. 19-20; Ps. 35; Mark 15
5   Ex. 21-22; Ps. 36; Mark 16
6   Ex. 23-24; Ps. 37; Luke 1
7   Ex. 25-26; Ps. 38; Luke 2
8   Ex. 27-28; Ps. 39; Luke 3
9   Ex. 29-30; Ps. 40; Luke 4
10 Ex. 31-32; Ps. 41; Luke 5
11 Ex. 33-34; Ps. 42; Luke 6
12 Ex. 35-36; Ps. 43; Luke 7
13 Ex. 37-38; Ps. 44; Luke 8
14 Ex. 39-40; Ps. 45; Luke 9
15 Lev. 1-2; Ps. 46; Luke 10
16 Lev. 3-4; Ps. 47; Luke 11
17 Lev. 5-6; Ps. 48; Luke 12
18 Lev. 7-8; Ps. 49; Luke 13
19 Lev. 9-10; Ps. 50; Luke 14
20 Lev. 11-12; Ps. 51; Luke 15
21 Lev. 13; Ps. 52; Luke 16
22 Lev. 14; Ps. 53; Luke 17
23 Lev. 15-16; Ps. 54; Luke 18
24 Lev. 17-18; Ps. 55; Luke 19
25 Lev. 19-20; Ps. 56; Luke 20
26 Lev. 21-22; Ps. 57; Luke 21
27 Lev. 23-24; Ps. 58; Luke 22
28 Lev. 25
29 Ps. 59; Luke 23

March

1   Lev. 26-27; Ps. 60; Luke 24
2   Num. 1-2; Ps. 61; John 1
3   Num. 3-4; Ps. 62; John 2-3
4   Num. 5-6; Ps. 63; John 4
5   Num. 7; Ps. 64; John 5
6   Num. 8-9; Ps. 65; John 6
7   Num. 10-11; Ps. 66; John 7
8   Num. 12-13; Ps. 67; John 8
9   Num. 14-15; Ps. 68; John 9
10 Num. 16; Ps. 69; John 10
11 Num. 17-18; Ps. 70; John 11
12 Num. 19-20; Ps. 71; John 12
13 Num. 21-22; Ps. 72; John 13
14 Num. 23-24; Ps. 73; John 14-15
15 Num. 25-26; Ps. 74; John 16
16 Num. 27-28; Ps. 75; John 17
17 Num. 29-30; Ps. 76; John 18
18 Num. 31-32; Ps. 77; John 19
19 Num. 33-34; Ps. 78; John 20
20 Num. 35-36; Ps. 79; John 21
21 Deut. 1-2; Ps. 80; Acts 1
22 Deut. 3-4; Ps. 81; Acts 2
23 Deut. 5-6; Ps. 82; Acts 3-4
24 Deut. 7-8; Ps. 83; Acts 5-6
25 Deut. 9-10; Ps. 84; Acts 7
26 Deut. 11-12; Ps. 85; Acts 8
27 Deut. 13-14; Ps. 86; Acts 9
28 Deut. 15-16; Ps. 87; Acts 10
29 Deut. 17-18; Ps. 88; Acts 11-12
30 Deut. 19-20; Ps. 89; Acts 13
31 Deut. 21-22; Ps. 90; Acts 14

April

1   Deut. 23-24; Ps. 91; Acts 15
2   Deut. 25-27; Ps. 92; Acts 16
3   Deut. 28-29; Ps. 93; Acts 17
4   Deut. 30-31; Ps. 94; Acts 18
5   Deut. 32; Ps. 95; Acts 19
6   Deut. 33-34; Ps. 96; Acts 20
7   Josh. 1-2; Ps. 97; Acts 21
8   Josh. 3-4; Ps. 98; Acts 22
9   Josh. 5-6; Ps. 99; Acts 23
10   Josh. 7-8; Ps. 100; Acts 24-25
11   Josh. 9-10; Ps. 101; Acts 26
12   Josh. 11-12; Ps. 102; Acts 27
13   Josh. 13-14; Ps. 103; Acts 28
14   Josh. 15-16; Ps. 104; Rom. 1-2
15   Josh. 17-18; Ps. 105; Rom. 3-4
16   Josh. 19-20; Ps. 106; Rom. 5-6
17   Josh. 21-22; Ps. 107; Rom. 7-8
18   Josh. 23-24; Ps. 108; Rom. 9-10
19   Judg. 1-2; Ps. 109; Rom. 11-12
20   Judg. 3-4; Ps. 110; Rom. 13-14
21   Judg. 5-6; Ps. 111; Rom. 15-16
22   Judg. 7-8; Ps. 112; 1 Cor. 1-2
23   Judg. 9; Ps. 113; 1 Cor. 3-4
24   Judg. 10-11; Ps. 114; 1 Cor. 5-6
25   Judg. 12-13; Ps. 115; 1 Cor. 7
26   Judg. 14-15; Ps. 116; 1 Cor. 8-9
27   Judg. 16-17; Ps. 117; 1 Cor. 10
28   Judg. 18-19; Ps. 118; 1 Cor. 11
29   Judg. 20-21; Ps. 119:1-88; 1 Cor. 12
30   Ruth 1-4; Ps. 119:89-176; 1 Cor. 13

May

1	1 Sam. 1-2; Ps. 120; 1 Cor. 14	
2	1 Sam. 3-4; Ps. 121; 1 Cor. 15	
3	1 Sam. 5-6; Ps. 122; 1 Cor. 16	
4	1 Sam. 7-8; Ps. 123; 2 Cor. 1	
5	1 Sam. 9-10; Ps. 124; 2 Cor. 2-3	
6	1 Sam. 11-12; Ps. 125; 2 Cor. 4-5	
7	1 Sam. 13-14; Ps. 126; 2 Cor. 6-7	
8	1 Sam. 15-16; Ps. 127; 2 Cor. 8	
9	1 Sam. 17; Ps. 128; 2 Cor. 9-10	
10	1 Sam. 18-19; Ps. 129; 2 Cor. 11	
11	1 Sam. 20-21; Ps. 130; 2 Cor. 12	
12	1 Sam. 22-23; Ps. 131; 2 Cor. 13	
13	1 Sam. 24-25; Ps. 132; Gal. 1-2	
14	1 Sam. 26-27; Ps. 133; Gal. 3-4	
15	1 Sam. 28-29; Ps. 134; Gal. 5-6	
16	1 Sam. 30-31; Ps. 135; Eph. 1-2	
17	2 Sam. 1-2; Ps. 136; Eph. 3-4	
18	2 Sam. 3-4; Ps. 137; Eph. 5-6	
19	2 Sam. 5-6; Ps. 138; Phil. 1-2	
20	2 Sam. 7-8; Ps. 139; Phil. 3-4	
21	2 Sam. 9-10; Ps. 140; Col. 1-2	
22	2 Sam. 11-12; Ps. 141; Col. 3-4	
23	2 Sam. 13-14; Ps. 142; 1 Thess. 1-2	
24	2 Sam. 15-16; Ps. 143; 1 Thess. 3-4	
25	2 Sam. 17-18; Ps. 144; 1 Thess. 5	
26	2 Sam. 19; Ps. 145; 2 Thess. 1-3	
27	2 Sam. 20-21; Ps. 146; 1 Tim. 1-2	
28	2 Sam. 22; Ps. 147; 1 Tim. 3-4	
29	2 Sam. 23-24; Ps. 148; 1 Tim. 5-6	
30	1 Kings 1; Ps. 149; 2 Tim. 1-2	
31	1 Kings 2-3; Ps. 150; 2 Tim. 3-4	

June

1   1 Kings 4-5; Prov. 1; Titus 1-3
2   1 Kings 6-7; Prov. 2; Philem.
3   1 Kings 8; Prov. 3; Heb. 1-2
4   1 Kings 9-10; Prov. 4; Heb. 3-4
5   1 Kings 11-12; Prov. 5; Heb. 5-6
6   1 Kings 13-14; Prov. 6; Heb. 7-8
7   1 Kings 15-16; Prov. 7; Heb. 9-10
8   1 Kings 17-18; Prov. 8; Heb. 11
9   1 Kings 19-20; Prov. 9; Heb. 12
10   1 Kings 21-22; Prov. 10; Heb. 13
11   2 Kings 1-2; Prov. 11; James 1
12   2 Kings 3-4; Prov. 12; James 2-3
13   2 Kings 5-6; Prov. 13; James 4-5
14   2 Kings 7-8; Prov. 14; 1 Pet. 1
15   2 Kings 9-10; Prov. 15; 1 Pet. 2-3
16   2 Kings 11-12; Prov. 16; 1 Pet. 4-5
17   2 Kings 13-14; Prov. 17; 2 Pet. 1-3
18   2 Kings 15-16; Prov. 18; 1 John 1-2
19   2 Kings 17; Prov. 19; 1 John 3-4
20   2 Kings 18-19; Prov. 20; 1 John 5
21   2 Kings 20-21; Prov. 21; 2 John
22   2 Kings 22-23; Prov. 22; 3 John
23   2 Kings 24-25; Prov. 23; Jude
24   1 Chron. 1; Prov. 24; Rev. 1-2
25   1 Chron. 2-3; Prov. 25; Rev. 3-5
26   1 Chron. 4-5; Prov. 26; Rev. 6-7
27   1 Chron. 6-7; Prov. 27; Rev. 8-10
28   1 Chron. 8-9; Prov. 28; Rev. 11-12
29   1 Chron. 10-11; Prov. 29; Rev. 13-14
30   1 Chron. 12-13; Prov. 30; Rev. 15-17

July

1   1 Chron. 14-15; Prov. 31; Rev. 18-19
2   1 Chron. 16-17; Ps. 1; Rev. 20-22
3   1 Chron. 18-19; Ps. 2; Matt. 1-2
4   1 Chron. 20-21; Ps. 3; Matt. 3-4
5   1 Chron. 22-23; Ps. 4; Matt. 5
6   1 Chron. 24-25; Ps. 5; Matt. 6-7
7   1 Chron. 26-27; Ps. 6; Matt. 8-9
8   1 Chron. 28-29; Ps. 7; Matt. 10-11
9   2 Chron. 1-2; Ps. 8; Matt. 12
10   2 Chron. 3-4; Ps. 9; Matt. 13
11   2 Chron. 5-6; Ps. 10; Matt. 14-15
12   2 Chron. 7-8; Ps. 11; Matt. 16-17
13   2 Chron. 9-10; Ps. 12; Matt. 18
14   2 Chron. 11-12; Ps. 13; Matt. 19-20
15   2 Chron. 13-14; Ps. 14; Matt. 21
16   2 Chron. 15-16; Ps. 15; Matt. 22
17   2 Chron. 17-18; Ps. 16; Matt. 23
18   2 Chron. 19-20; Ps. 17; Matt. 24
19   2 Chron. 21-22; Ps. 18; Matt. 25
20   2 Chron. 23-24; Ps. 19; Matt. 26
21   2 Chron. 25-26; Ps. 20; Matt. 27
22   2 Chron. 27-28; Ps. 21; Matt. 28
23   2 Chron. 29-30; Ps. 22; Mark 1
24   2 Chron. 31-32; Ps. 23; Mark 2
25   2 Chron. 33-34; Ps. 24; Mark 3
26   2 Chron. 35-36; Ps. 25; Mark 4
27   Ezra 1-2; Ps. 26; Mark 5
28   Ezra 3-4; Ps. 27; Mark 6
29   Ezra 5-6; Ps. 28; Mark 7
30   Ezra 7-8; Ps. 29; Mark 8
31   Ezra 9-10; Ps. 30; Mark 9

August

1   Neh. 1-2; Ps. 31; Mark 10
2   Neh. 3-4; Ps. 32; Mark 11
3   Neh. 5-6; Ps. 33; Mark 12
4   Neh. 7, Ps. 34; Mark 13
5   Neh. 8-9; Ps. 35; Mark 14
6   Neh. 10-11; Ps. 36; Mark 15
7   Neh. 12-13; Ps. 37; Mark 16
8   Esth. 1-2; Ps. 38; Luke 1
9   Esth. 3-4; Ps. 39; Luke 2
10 Esth. 5-6; Ps. 40; Luke 3
11 Esth. 7-8; Ps. 41; Luke 4
12 Esth. 9-10; Ps. 42; Luke 5
13 Job 1-2; Ps. 43; Luke 6
14 Job 3-4; Ps. 44; Luke 7
15 Job 5-6; Ps. 45; Luke 8
16 Job 7-8; Ps. 46; Luke 9
17 Job 9-10; Ps. 47; Luke 10
18 Job 11-12; Ps. 48; Luke 11
19 Job 13-14; Ps. 49; Luke 12
20 Job 15-16; Ps. 50; Luke 13
21 Job 17-18; Ps. 51; Luke 14
22 Job 19-20; Ps. 52; Luke 15
23 Job 21-22; Ps. 53; Luke 16
24 Job 23-25; Ps. 54; Luke 17
25 Job 26-28; Ps. 55; Luke 18
26 Job 29-30; Ps. 56; Luke 19
27 Job 31-32; Ps. 57; Luke 20
28 Job 33-34; Ps. 58; Luke 21
29 Job 35-36; Ps. 59; Luke 22
30 Job 37-38; Ps. 60; Luke 23
31 Job 39-40; Ps. 61; Luke 24

September

1   Job 41-42; Ps. 62; John 1
2   Eccl. 1-2; Ps. 63; John 2-3
3   Eccl. 3-4; Ps. 64; John 4
4   Eccl. 5-6; Ps. 65; John 5
5   Eccl. 7-8; Ps. 66; John 6
6   Eccl. 9-10; Ps. 67; John 7
7   Eccl. 11-12; Ps. 68; John 8
8   Song of Sol. 1-2; Ps. 69; John 9
9   Song of Sol. 3-4; Ps. 70; John 10
10 Song of Sol. 5-6; Ps. 71; John 11
11 Song of Sol. 7-8; Ps. 72; John 12
12 Isaiah 1-2; Ps. 73; John 13
13 Isaiah 3-5; Ps. 74; John 14-15
14 Isaiah 6-8; Ps. 75; John 16
15 Isaiah 9-10; Ps. 76; John 17
16 Isaiah 11-13; Ps. 77; John 18
17 Isaiah 14-15; Ps. 78; John 19
18 Isaiah 16-17; Ps. 79; John 20
19 Isaiah 18-19; Ps. 80; John 21
20 Isaiah 20-22; Ps. 81; Acts 1
21 Isaiah 23-24; Ps. 82; Acts 2
22 Isaiah 25-26; Ps. 83; Acts 3-4
23 Isaiah 27-28; Ps. 84; Acts 5-6
24 Isaiah 29-30; Ps. 85; Acts 7
25 Isaiah 31-32; Ps. 86; Acts 8
26 Isaiah 33-34; Ps. 87; Acts 9
27 Isaiah 35-36; Ps. 88; Acts 10
28 Isaiah 37-38; Ps. 89; Acts 11-12
29 Isaiah 39-40; Ps. 90; Acts 13
30 Isaiah 41-42; Ps. 91; Acts 14

October

1   Isaiah 43-44; Ps. 92; Acts 15
2   Isaiah 45-46; Ps. 93; Acts 16
3   Isaiah 47-48; Ps. 94; Acts 17
4   Isaiah 49-50; Ps. 95; Acts 18
5   Isaiah 51-52; Ps. 96; Acts 19
6   Isaiah 53-54; Ps. 97; Acts 20
7   Isaiah 55-56; Ps. 98; Acts 21
8   Isaiah 57-58; Ps. 99; Acts 22
9   Isaiah 59-60; Ps. 100; Acts 23
10 Isaiah 61-62; Ps. 101; Acts 24-25
11 Isaiah 63-64; Ps. 102; Acts 26
12 Isaiah 65-66; Ps. 103; Acts 27
13 Jer. 1-2; Ps. 104; Acts 28
14 Jer. 3-4; Ps. 105; Rom. 1-2
15 Jer. 5-6; Ps. 106; Rom. 3-4
16 Jer. 7-8; Ps. 107; Rom. 5-6
17 Jer. 9-10; Ps. 108; Rom. 7-8
18 Jer. 11-12; Ps. 109; Rom. 9-10
19 Jer. 13-14; Ps. 110; Rom. 11-12
20 Jer. 15-16; Ps. 111; Rom. 13-14
21 Jer. 17-18; Ps. 112; Rom. 15-16
22 Jer. 19-20; Ps. 113; 1 Cor. 1-2
23 Jer. 21-22; Ps. 114; 1 Cor. 3-4
24 Jer. 23-24; Ps. 115; 1 Cor. 5-6
25 Jer. 25-26; Ps. 116; 1 Cor. 7
26 Jer. 27-28; Ps. 117; 1 Cor. 8-9
27 Jer. 29-30; Ps. 118; 1 Cor. 10
28 Jer. 31-32; Ps. 119:1-64; 1 Cor. 11
29 Jer. 33-34; Ps. 119:65-120; 1 Cor. 12
30 Jer. 35-36; Ps. 119:121-176; 1 Cor. 13
31 Jer. 37-38; Ps. 120; 1 Cor. 14

November

1   Jer. 39-40; Ps. 121; 1 Cor. 15
2   Jer. 41-42; Ps. 122; 1 Cor. 16
3   Jer. 43-44; Ps. 123; 2 Cor. 1
4   Jer. 45-46; Ps. 124; 2 Cor. 2-3
5   Jer. 47-48; Ps. 125; 2 Cor. 4-5
6   Jer. 49-50; Ps. 126; 2 Cor. 6-7
7   Jer. 51-52; Ps. 127; 2 Cor. 8
8   Lam. 1-2; Ps. 128; 2 Cor. 9-10
9   Lam. 3; Ps. 129; 2 Cor. 11
10   Lam. 4-5; Ps. 130; 2 Cor. 12
11   Ezek. 1-2; Ps. 131; 2 Cor. 13
12   Ezek. 3-4; Ps. 132; Gal. 1-2
13   Ezek. 5-6; Ps. 133; Gal. 3-4
14   Ezek. 7-8; Ps. 134; Gal. 5-6
15   Ezek. 9-10; Ps. 135; Eph. 1-2
16   Ezek. 11-12; Ps. 136; Eph. 3-4
17   Ezek. 13-14; Ps. 137; Eph. 5-6
18   Ezek. 15-16; Ps. 138; Phil. 1-2
19   Ezek. 17-18; Ps. 139; Phil. 3-4
20   Ezek. 19-20; Ps. 140; Col. 1-2
21   Ezek. 21-22; Ps. 141; Col. 3-4
22   Ezek. 23-24; Ps. 142; 1 Thess. 1-2
23   Ezek. 25-26; Ps. 143; 1 Thess. 3-4
24   Ezek. 27-28; Ps. 144; 1 Thess. 5
25   Ezek. 29-30; Ps. 145; 2 Thess. 1-3
26   Ezek. 31-32; Ps. 146; 1 Tim. 1-2
27   Ezek. 33-34; Ps. 147; 1 Tim. 3-4
28   Ezek. 35-36; Ps. 148; 1 Tim. 5-6
29   Ezek. 37-38; Ps. 149; 2 Tim. 1-2
30   Ezek. 39-40; Ps. 150; 2 Tim. 3-4